Aegean Whispers: Kusadası's Charm

Moni Arora

COPYRIGHT INFORMATION

ISBN: 978-1-3999-7401-1

DEDICATION

This book is dedicated to the people of Kusadası, whose spirit and generosity have made it possible to capture the essence of this enchanting place – a place where history and modernity dance together, where the sunsets over the Aegean are not just a spectacle, but a testament to the enduring magic that is Kusadası.

ACKNOWLEDGEMENT

To my family, friends and colleagues who provided countless hours of discussion and feedback, your contribution has been invaluable.

A sincere acknowledgement to those extraordinary individuals who went above and beyond, lending their expertise, encouragement, and unwavering support.

Ecehan Dolgun (Kusadası Belediyesi)
Dilara Kılıc (Kusadası Belediyesi)
Paulina Maruszewska
Murat Soykan (Murat Studio)
Omer Calıskan (Adonis Travel)
Lucy Arora
Berkant Akbacak
Mehmet Zorlu
Mesut Gonenc
Serdar Gurel

Special thanks to my editor, Amy Arora, whose keen eye for detail and relentless pursuit of excellence pushed this work to new heights.

Finally, I want to express my heartfelt appreciation to my readers. It's your curiosity, engagement, and passion for learning about this paradise called Kusadası that motivated me to write this book. I hope this book inspires you as much as you inspire me to continue to spread the word about Kusadası's charm.

Check out Kusadasi Life YouTube Channel @KusadasiLife

YouTube Channel: @KusadasıLife
Website: www.KusadasıLife.net
Email: moni@Kusadasılife.net

CONTENT

Foreward

As I stepped off the plane in Izmir for what was meant to be just another holiday, I had no idea that the coastal town of Kusadası would capture my heart and become my home for the next 18 years. The warm sun on my face and the gentle breeze carrying the scent of the sea were the first signs that I had discovered a hidden gem on Turkey's Aegean coast.

My love for Kusadası grew with each day I spent exploring its rich history, vibrant culture, and breathtaking natural beauty. From the ancient ruins of Ephesus to the lively bazaars and bustling marina, I found myself immersed in a world where the past and present coexist in perfect harmony.

As the years went by, I decided to share my passion for Kusadası with others through my YouTube Channel, @KusadasıLife, and my website, www.KusadasıLife.net. By showcasing the town's many attractions, local events, and hidden gems, I hoped to inspire fellow travellers to embark on their own Kusadası adventure.

I am thrilled at the opportunity to share my love for Kusadası with an even wider audience. This comprehensive guide provides invaluable insights and insider tips for anyone looking to explore the town's history, culture, and natural wonders.

As you delve into the pages of this book, I hope you will be inspired to experience Kusadası's captivating charm for yourself. Whether you're planning your first visit or seeking new adventures in a familiar setting, let this guide be your companion as you uncover the magic of Kusadası and create memories that will last a lifetime.

With warmest regards,

Moni Arora
Kusadası Enthusiast & Resident YouTube
Channel: @KusadasıLife
Website: www.KusadasıLife.net
Email: moni@Kusadasılife.net

INTRODUCTION

The Allure of Kusadası and its Coastal Charm

Kusadası, a picturesque seaside town on Turkey's Aegean coast, captivates travellers with its breathtaking scenery, crystal-clear waters, and welcoming atmosphere. Its coastal charm is amplified by its vibrant culture, lively streets, and delicious culinary offerings, making it an ideal destination for those seeking both relaxation and adventure. The town is a gateway to the region's rich history, with countless ancient ruins and cultural sites dotting the surrounding landscape. Kusadası's unique blend of natural beauty and historical significance has made it a favourite among travellers from around the world.

A Brief Overview of Kusadası's History, Culture, and Natural Beauty

The history of Kusadası dates back thousands of years, with civilizations such as the Ionians, Romans, Byzantines, and Ottomans leaving their mark on the area. Throughout its storied past, Kusadası has played a significant role as a port city and a centre of trade, leaving behind a wealth of historical sites and artefacts that offer a glimpse into the lives of those who once inhabited the region.

Kusadası's culture is a delightful fusion of ancient traditions and modern influences. Visitors can immerse themselves in the town's rich cultural heritage by exploring its museums, monuments, and ancient ruins, while also enjoying its contemporary art, music, and entertainment scenes.

The town's natural beauty is an integral part of its allure, with stunning beaches, lush national parks, and nearby islands offering countless opportunities for outdoor exploration and relaxation. Kusadası's picturesque coastline, with its turquoise waters and golden sands, invites visitors to unwind and soak up the sun, while its surrounding landscapes provide a wealth of adventure for nature enthusiasts and thrill-seekers alike.

The book's purpose and structure

Throughout this book, our aim is to provide you with the knowledge and inspiration needed to embark on your own Kusadası adventure. In the chapters that follow, we will delve deeper into the many facets of Kusadası, providing a comprehensive guide to the town's history, culture, attractions, and hidden gems. Whether you're a first-time visitor or a seasoned traveller returning to this captivating seaside town, we hope that this guide will help you uncover new experiences and create unforgettable memories in Kusadası, a true gem on Turkey's Aegean coast.

CHAPTER 1
A Storied Past: Kusadası's Rich History

1.1 Prehistoric settlements in the region

Long before Kuşadası's breathtaking coastline became a sought after destination for tourists from every corner of the globe, the area played host to prehistoric settlements that thrived in the embrace of its fertile lands and generous waters. In their investigations, archaeologists have unearthed a treasure trove of artefacts and remnants in the region, painting a vivid portrait of the lives and dreams of those who first called this enchanting landscape home.

Dating back to the Neolithic period, these early agricultural communities laid the groundwork for the rich tapestry of culture and heritage that defines Kusadası today. As the sun came up, these ancient inhabitants would rise, tilling the soil and nurturing the seeds that would, in time, yield a bountiful harvest. They understood the delicate balance of nature and worked in harmony with the land, ensuring the prosperity of their families and communities.

With the sparkling waters of the Aegean Sea as their constant companion, the early settlers of Kusadası also turned to the ocean for sustenance. Casting their nets beneath the shimmering waves, they forged a deep connection with the sea, which provided them with an abundant array of fish and seafood to nourish both their bodies and their spirits. Through their intimate relationship with the natural world, these pioneers laid the foundation for the thriving coastal communities that still exist today.

As you stroll along the sun-drenched shores of Kusadası or explore the streets of its ancient cities, take a moment to reflect on the legacy of these early settlers.

1.2 The hidden connection: The ancient city of Neapolis and Kusadası

Located at the crossroads of the Aegean and Mediterranean, Turkey is a mosaic of cultures and civilizations, its history traced back to the earliest human settlements.

From the Hittites to the Ottomans, the region has seen the rise and fall of many powerful empires, leaving behind a remarkable architectural heritage. Two examples of this historical legacy are the ancient city of Neapolis and the modern-day city of Kusadası, which share an intriguing connection.

Neapolis, meaning 'New City' in Greek, was a common name for many cities during the Hellenistic period. The Neapolis we are referring to was located in the Anatolian region and was a significant hub during the Roman era. The exact location of Neapolis has been a subject of debate among historians, with some suggesting that it was situated in what is now modern-day Kusadası.

Historical records show that the city of Neapolis was built around the 2nd century BC. It was a prominent maritime city due to its strategic location and prospered greatly during the Roman era. Its importance can be seen from the numerous archaeological remains, such as the Roman aqueducts, amphitheatres, and bathhouses.

The connection between Neapolis and Kusadası comes to light when we look at historical maps and archaeological evidence. Ancient maps and texts reference a city near the Aegean coast, bearing features that match the geographical layout of present-day Kusadası. Furthermore, archaeological excavations in and around Kusadası have unearthed artefacts and structures that align with the Roman era when Neapolis flourished.

Most notably, the unearthing of a large Roman bath complex in Kusadası hints at the town's Roman past. This bath complex, characteristic of the Roman era, is similar to those found in other parts of Neapolis, suggesting a shared architectural style and urban planning.

Moreover, ancient coins discovered in Kusadası bear the name Neapolis, suggesting the city's existence in this location. The discovery of these artefacts has led historians and archaeologists to theorize that Kusadası could, in fact, be the site of the ancient city of Neapolis.

Another link between Neapolis and Kusadası is their shared maritime tradition. As a port city, Neapolis was a hub for maritime trade and transportation in the Roman era. Similarly, Kusadası's modern harbour serves as an important port for international cruises and local fishing vessels.

Although there may not be a direct, indisputable link establishing Kusadası as the exact location of the ancient city of Neapolis, the archaeological discoveries, geographical similarities, and shared maritime tradition suggest a fascinating connection between the two. This connection serves as a reminder of the layered history of this region and its continual evolution from the ancient world to the present day.

1.3 Byzantine Era: Kusadası's strategic role

As the sun set on the Roman Empire, giving rise to the Byzantine Empire, Kusadası, then known as 'Ania', continued to be seen as a shining jewel along the Aegean coast. With the tide of history shifting, the Byzantine era heralded the construction of numerous formidable fortifications, including the majestic Kusadası Castle, which still proudly stands sentinel over the city's shores to this day.

These imposing defensive structures, forged by the skill and determination of Byzantine architects and masons, played a crucial role in safeguarding Kusadası from the ever-present threat of pirate raids and invasions. Their towering walls and watchful ramparts served as a bulwark against the chaos of a world in flux, ensuring the city's survival and prosperity.

During this turbulent time, Kusadası also emerged as a significant waypoint for Christian pilgrims embarking on their sacred journey to the nearby ancient city of Ephesus, a treasure trove of holy sites and relics. Home to the House of the Virgin Mary and other revered landmarks, Ephesus became a beacon of hope, faith, and spiritual solace for countless devoted souls who travelled from far and wide to draw closer to the divine.

From the towering ramparts of Kusadası Castle to the echoes of pilgrims' footsteps that still linger in the air, Kusadası's past weaves a timeless tale of courage, devotion, and the indomitable spirit of humanity in the face of adversity.

1.4 Ottoman Empire: a period of growth and prosperity

Kusadası's significance surged when it was embraced by the mighty Ottoman Empire in the 15th century. Perceiving the strategic value of Kusadası's prime location, the Ottomans wasted no time in investing heavily in the development of its port facilities. This ambitious expansion fortified Kusadası's role as an indispensable trading post, weaving an intricate web of connections between the empire, the Mediterranean, and the far reaches of the known world.

As the 16th and 17th centuries unfurled, Kusadası blossomed under the protection of the Ottoman Empire. The city's population swelled as individuals from a diverse array of ethnic backgrounds – Turks, Greeks, Armenians, and Jews – flocked to its lively streets, drawn by the promise of prosperity and opportunity that Kusadası offered.

In this melting pot of cultures and dreams, Kusadası's eclectic character took root, as people from all walks of life shared their customs, beliefs, and stories with one another. Art, music, and culinary traditions intermingled, uniting hearts and erasing borders.

Today, Kusadası's energetic spirit endures, a testament to the power of diversity, collaboration, and mutual understanding. As you wander through this special city, embrace the legacy of those who came before you, and in doing so, forge a connection to the past that will forever enrich your experience of this remarkable corner of the world.

1.5 The modern era: transition to a tourist hub

As the curtain fell on the Ottoman Empire and the fledgling Republic of Turkey emerged, Kusadası continued to grow and adapt, its spirit as unyielding as the waves that caress its sun-kissed shores.

The winds of change whispered through the city's streets in the 20th century, as Kusadası's economic focus pivoted from trade to the burgeoning world of tourism.

Soon, Kusadası beckoned to holiday-makers from every corner of the globe, its allure undeniable and irresistible. As the world took notice,the city embarked on a transformative journey, with modern hotels, resorts, and infrastructure rising from the sands to welcome travellers in search of adventure, relaxation, and discovery.

In a delicate dance of past and present, Kusadası has managed tostrike a harmonious balance between preserving its storied history and embracing the needs of contemporary travellers. This enchanting fusion is the lifeblood of Kusadası, a place where time-honoured traditions and modern innovation intertwine, creating a captivating destination that defies definition.

1000+ Cruise Ships Arrive in Kusadası Every Year

Whether you're drawn by its history, its people, or the promise of unforgettable adventures, Kusadası waits with open arms, ready to reveal the countless wonders that lie within its heart.

Gazi Beğendi

CHAPTER 2
Sunrise to Sunset: A Day in the Life of Kusadası

2.1 Morning routines and local markets

As the sun rises over the Aegean, casting its warm rays on Kusadası, the town comes alive with the energy of locals beginning their day. The smell of freshly baked simit, a sesame-crusted bread ring that's crispy on the outside and soft on the inside, fills the air as bakeries open their doors for business. Many locals break their fast with a steaming cup of cay (Turkish tea) accompanied by olives, cheese, and tomatoes as they engage in friendly conversation with neighbours.

Cay (Turkish tea)

The bustling marketplaces in Kusadası are a hive of activity. Every week, locals throng to the open-air bazaar to browse the stalls selling handmade goods, fragrant spices, and fresh produce. These markets serve as both a location to shop and a gathering spot for people to catch up on the newest rumours and news.

2.2 Afternoon activities: beaches and sightseeing

As the day progresses, the town's idyllic beaches fill with sun- seekers eager to bask in the warm Mediterranean climate. Families and friends gather on the golden sands of Ladies Beach and Long Beach, sharing picnics and enjoying the sparkling waters.

For those seeking culture and history, Kusadası offers a plethora of sightseeing opportunities. Visitors can explore the ancient ruins of Ephesus or wander the narrow streets of Kaleici, Kusadası's old town, admiring the charming Ottoman-era houses and Kervansaray, once an inn for travelling merchants.

2.3 Evening entertainment: dining and nightlife options

As the sun begins to set, Kusadası's nightlife awakens. Locals and tourists alike gather at waterfront restaurants, indulging in mouthwatering meze platters and succulent seafood while sipping on raki, Turkey's aniseed-flavored spirit. The atmosphere is lively, with the clinking of glasses and the warm hum of conversation filling the air.

For those looking to dance the night away, Kusadası's bars and nightclubs offer a variety of music and entertainment options. From traditional Turkish live music to international DJ sets, there's something for everyone.

2.4 The role of family and community in daily life

Family and community are an important part of Kusadası life. Multi-generational families can be seen sharing meals and enjoying leisure time together, while neighbours exchange pleasantries and help one another with daily tasks. The community spirit, along with the warmth and hospitality, is what brings visitors back to Kusadası again and again.

CHAPTER 3
Coastal Cuisine: Savouring Kusadası's Culinary Delights

3.1 Breakfast staples: simit, borek, and menemen

The culinary journey through Kusadası begins with a traditional Turkish breakfast, or kahvaltı, which is a delightful assortment of flavours and textures. Locals often begin their day with simit paired with creamy white cheese, ripe tomatoes, and olives. Yum! Now that's a satisfying start to the day.

Simit

Borek, another breakfast favourite, is a flaky pastry typically filled with cheese, spinach, or minced meat. These savoury pastries are available in various shapes and sizes, each offering a unique combination of flavours. Menemen, a popular scrambled egg dish, is cooked with tomatoes, green peppers, and onions, creating a hearty and flavourful meal which is loved by many.

Borek

3.2 Local seafood dishes: grilled fish and calamari

Kusadası's prime location along the Aegean coast means that fresh seafood is a staple in the local diet. Grilled fish, such as sea bass or red mullet, is often served whole, drizzled with olive oil and sprinkled with herbs and lemon juice. The succulent, tender flesh pairs beautifully with crisp mixed greens or a simple tomato and cucumber salad.

Fried calamari is another coastal favourite, with tender squid rings coated in a light, golden batter. Enjoy them with a squeeze of lemon and a dollop of garlicky yogurt sauce for a delectable treat.

3.3 Meze culture: sampling small plates

Meze is an integral part of Kusadası's culinary culture, offering a delightful way to sample a range of dishes. Goodbye food envy! These small plates, which can be hot or cold, are meant to be shared and savoured among friends and family. Popular meze dishes include patlıcan salatası (smoky eggplant salad), cacık (yogurt with cucumber and mint), and dolma (stuffed vine leaves).

An essential component of any meze spread is freshly baked pide, a boat-shaped flatbread that's perfect for scooping up flavourful dips and sauces. Whether enjoyed as a light meal or a prelude to a larger feast, meze captures the spirit of Kusadası's friendly dining culture.

Assortment of Meze

3.4 Traditional Turkish desserts and beverages

No culinary tour of Kusadası would be complete without indulging in some of Turkey's famous desserts. Baklava, a sweet pastry made from layers of thin, buttery filo dough filled with chopped nuts and drenched in syrup, is a must-try. Lokum, or Turkish delight, is another classic, offering a variety of flavours and textures, from rosewater-scented cubes to pistachio-studded rolls.

To accompany these sweet treats, sip on a cup of rich, velvety Turkish coffee or a glass of refreshing ayran, a frothy yogurt-based drink that helps to cleanse the palate.

Baklava

3.5 Culinary experiences: cooking classes and food tours

For those looking to immerse themselves in Kusadası's culinary scene, cooking classes and food tours offer hands-on opportunities to learn about local ingredients, techniques, and traditions. Local chefs and passionate home cooks teach visitors how to prepare classic Turkish dishes, while food tours introduce travellers to Kusadası's best eateries, markets, and street food vendors.

Cooking classes in Kusadası provide a unique opportunity to learn traditional recipes passed down through generations. Participants can master the art of making manti, a type of Turkish dumpling, or learn the secrets behind crafting the perfect baklava. These classes often include visits to local markets, where visitors can learn about the importance of seasonal ingredients and experience the electrifying atmosphere of Kusadası's busy bazaars.

Food tours, on the other hand, offer an immersive journey through the flavours and aromas that define Kusadası's culinary landscape. Led by knowledgeable guides, these tours take visitors on a gastronomic adventure, sampling dishes from street food vendors, family-owned eateries, and high-end restaurants. Along the way, participants will gain insights into the local culture, history, and culinary traditions that make Kusadası's food scene so captivating.

From savouring local delicacies at the weekly bazaar to mastering the art of Turkish cooking, Kusadası's culinary experiences provide a unique and delicious way to connect with the town's special heritage.

CHAPTER 4

Adventures on the Aegean: Exploring Kusadası's Seaside Activities

4.1 Kusadası's best beaches: Ladies Beach, Long Beach, and others

With its sun-soaked coastline, Kusadası offers plenty of beautiful beaches for visitors to enjoy. Here are a few popular beaches:

Kusadası Downtown Beach

Nestled along the city's main promenade, the Downtown Beach near the marina offers a quaint seaside escape. Though compact, its sandy shores and calm, shallow waters provide a relaxing atmosphere. While sunbeds are scarce, early birds can secure a spot under available umbrellas. The beach treats visitors to stunning views of the city, Pigeon Island fortress, and the bustling harbour. Its proximity to a lively Marina area filled with restaurants and shops ensures easy access to amenities, making it a perfect spot for a quick beach getaway with a side of city charm.

Kusadası Downtown Beach

Ladies Beach

A stone's throw away from the heart of the city, Ladies Beach is one of Kusadası's most popular beaches, drawing many visitors. The name originates from its past as a beach exclusively for women. Nowadays, everyone is welcome to take part in the numerous water activities, sunbathing, and café culture. The pristine water is perfect for swimming and the shallow waters make it an ideal choice for families with young children. Nearby eateries and bars cater to those looking to unwind with a cool drink or snack.

Ladies Beach

Lost Paradise Beach

A brief drive from Kusadası leads to this spectacular beach, surrounded on all sides by greenery and clear waters. Escape the throngs and enjoy a peaceful day by the sea, with various water sports, sunbeds, and cafés at your disposal.

Lost Paradise Beach

Green Beach

Green Beach is located in a small bay close to the Grand Blue Sky International Hotel in Ladies Beach, ten minutes from Kusadası town centre. Green Beach is conveniently accessible by car or the number 5 minibus, which travels through the heart of Kusadası.

Previously open to the public, Green Beach is now home to one of Kusadası's newest beach clubs. The Green Beach family club is on three levels and has a large restaurant where you can eat breakfast or lunch without getting off the beach. Green Beach is a popular place with local and foreign tourists.

Green Beach

Okul Beach

Okul Beach is located right next to Green Beach Family Club in the Ladies Beach area. Okul beach is much smaller beach than Green Beach however all the facilities such as sun loungers, umbrellas, showers and toilets are provided for a small fee. There is also a restaurant where you can enjoy food and drinks.

Okul Beach

Long Beach

True to its name, Long Beach boasts an extensive sandy coastline ideal for walking, jogging, and sunbathing. Long Beach, stretching over 18 kilometres, offers a more tranquil setting for those seeking peace and relaxation. It's also a popular spot for windsurfing and kitesurfing, thanks to the strong winds. The expansive coastline provides ample space for sunbathing, beach sports, and leisurely strolls along the shore. Restaurants and cafés on the waterfront serve up delicious food and beverages, making it an excellent spot to spend the day.

Long Beach

Diamond Sand Beach

Diamond Sand Beach is a mesmerizing coastal haven nestled along the Aegean Sea on Long Beach. This beach, well-known for its golden, powder-soft sands that glitter like diamonds in the sun, provides a peaceful haven for those looking to escape it all and take in the scenery. The crystal clear waters gently caress the shore, inviting visitors to indulge in leisurely swims or bask in the sun on the pristine sands. Diamond Sand Beach is where visitors can unwind, rejuvenate, and savour the enchanting essence of the Turkish coastline.

Diamond Sand Beach

Star Beach

For beachgoers looking to escape the crowds and have a quiet day at the shore, Star Beach, located on Long Beach next to Dream Beach, is the ideal location. Stunning views of the Greek island of Samos and the National Park, along with crystal-clear, turquoise waters, entice guests to enjoy leisurely swims or sunbathing on the immaculate dunes. You can stay on the beach since Star Beach restaurant serves food and beverages.

Star Beach

Dream Beach

Dream Beach is Located next to Star Beach and has a bigger sea frontage than Star Beach. Also, the restaurant at Dream Beach is bigger providing more seating facilities. Dream Beach, like Star Beach, also has amazing views of the Greek island of Samos and the Dilek Peninsula. Dream Beach is a perfect place to get away from it all and enjoy sunbathing or leisurely swims while drinking your favourite beverage or enjoying a meal from the Dream Beach restaurant.

Dream Beach

Sevgi Plaji

Sevgi Plaji is the perfect beach for people who want to escape the crowds. It's both calm and remote. With fine sand, calm waters, and clear views of the Aegean Sea, this beach is enveloped by lush vegetation, making it a favourite spot for picnics and barbecues.

Sevgi Plaji

Kustur Beach

This gorgeous sandy beach is conveniently located near Kusadası and features a range of water activities, sunbeds, and cafés. The clear water is perfect for swimming, while nearby restaurants and bars cater to those looking to enjoy a refreshing drink or snack.

Kustur Beach

Pamucak Beach

As a sought-after destination in Kusadası, Turkey, Pamucak Beach is famed for its golden sands and transparent waters, making it perfect for sunbathing, swimming, and water sports. It provides a spectacular view of the Aegean Sea as well as the surrounding vegetation. Facilities include sunbeds, umbrellas, showers, and restaurants. Pamucak Beach is a must- visit for anyone seeking a relaxing and picturesque beach experience.

Pamucak Beach

Yilanci Burnu Beach or Snake Island
(Don't worry there are no snakes!)

Don't worry there are no snakes! Yilanci Burnu is located close to Kusadası Harbour and has great views of the harbour and the cruise ships. Yilanci Burnu has striking rock formations and clear waters. Yilanci Burnu is a popular destination for swimming, sunbathing, and snorkelling.

Yilanci Burnu Beach

Other notable beaches include the pristine beaches at **Dilek Peninsula**, within a beautiful national park.

4.2 Water sports: windsurfing, Jet Skiing, and parasailing
Windsurfing

Kusadası presents adrenaline enthusiasts with an irresistible combination of clear waters and dependable winds, which makes it the perfect place for a range of thrilling water sports. Those eager to harness the power of the wind can dive into windsurfing, with equipment rentals and lessons available to transform novices into skilled surfers. As the breeze propels you across the sparkling waters, you'll feel a surge of excitement and freedom.

Windsurfing

Jet Skiing

For a high-octane adventure, Jet Skiing offers an unparalleled way to discover Kusadası's beautiful coastline. Feel the wind whip through your hair as you zip across the waves, the powerful engine roaring beneath you. With an incredible sense of control and exhilaration, Jet Skiing allows you to experience Kusadası's azure waters from a unique perspective.

Jet Skiing

Parasailing

For those who dream of soaring high, parasailing grants a bird's- eye view of the awe-inspiring scenery below. Safely strapped into a parachute harness, you'll be gently lifted into the sky, suspended from a speedboat that cruises through the sparkling sea. As you glide effortlessly through the air, your heart will race with anticipation and wonder, taking in the captivating vistas of Kusadası's shoreline and surrounding landscapes.

Parasailing

Embrace the thrill of aquatic adventures in Kusadası and create memories to share with your loved ones once you get home.

4.3 Boat tours and yacht charters: exploring nearby islands

The coastal beauty of Kusadası is best seen on a voyage by boat. Local tour operators eagerly await, ready to whisk you away on daily excursions to the enchanting nearby islands and secluded bays. A boat tour allows visitors to uncover secret spots, such as pristine beaches and crystal- clear swimming spots, that are otherwise inaccessible.

To elevate your seafaring adventure, chartering a private yacht or a gulet —a traditional wooden sailing vessel—promises a more bespoke and intimate experience. Revel in the luxury and privacy of your very own aquatic haven, as you glide across the shimmering seas. These exclusive charters typically come with an experienced crew and a knowledgeable captain, ensuring not only a safe and comfortable journey but also a customizable one. Your personal captain will gladly tailor the itinerary to suit your preferences and interests, crafting an unforgettable voyage that caters specifically to your desires.

Embrace the enchantment of Kusadası's coastal beauty and embark on a mesmerising journey by boat. Whether you choose a guided tour or a private charter, you'll be spellbound by the wonders that you'll see along the stunning shores of this Turkish paradise.

4.4 Underwater exploration: top snorkelling and diving sites

It's not just the sun-kissed shores that are worth a look. Underwater exploration is an essential part of any visit to Kusadası. The warm, crystalline waters of the Aegean Sea cradle a vast array of marine life, ranging from vividly-hued fish and graceful sea turtles to the occasional playful dolphin. Snorkelling and diving aficionados are in for a true treat as they embark on an aquatic adventure, visiting both shallow, vivacious reefs and deeper, more mysterious locations, such as the Adabanko Reef and Baradin Bay.

As you immerse yourself in this enchanting world beneath the waves, you'll marvel at the kaleidoscope of colours, the delicate dance of marine creatures, and the serene sense of wonder that envelops you. It's unforgettable!

A multitude of PADI-certified dive centres in Kusadası cater to underwater explorers of all skill levels, providing equipment rentals and guided dives to ensure a secure and delightful dive into the depths. Friendly and knowledgeable instructors will be your trusted companions, sharing their expertise and passion for the magical marine world that awaits you.

Kusadası is truly a paradise for beach lovers and water sports enthusiasts alike. From tranquil sunbathing spots to thrilling water adventures, the town's coastal attractions cater to a wide range of tastes and interests.

CHAPTER 5
Things to do in Kusadası

5.1 Unforgettable tours and excursions around Kusadası
Turkish bath (Hamam)

Immerse yourself in a centuries-old Turkish tradition by indulging in a hamam. This rejuvenating experience starts with a steam bath to open your pores, followed by a full body scrub, and finally a soothing massage. It's the perfect way to relax and unwind after a day of sightseeing.

Greek Island of Samos

A trip to Samos, a Greek Island: Take a ferry to the charming Greek island of Samos, just a short trip from Kusadası. Explore its picturesque villages, swim in the azure waters, and sample delicious Greek cuisine. Don't forget to try the famous Samos wine!

Pythagorion, Samos!

Pythagorio

Waterparks: Adaland and Aqua Fantasy

For a fun-filled day, head to Adaland or Aqua Fantasy, two of the largest water parks in Europe. With a variety of slides, pools, and attractions, these parks offer entertainment for all ages.

Aqua Fantasy

Quad Safari

For an adrenaline-fueled adventure, join a quad safari and navigate through pine forests, rural paths, and sandy beaches. It's a thrilling way to explore the Kusadası countryside.

Quad Safari

Buggy Safari

For a more intimate off-road experience, a buggy safari offers a blend of adventure and nature as you drive through the rugged landscapes around Kusadası.

Buggy Safari

Jeep Safari

Hop on a jeep safari for a day of off-road exploration. The safari takes you through mountainous terrain, charming villages, and scenic vistas, all of which surround Kusadası.

Jeep Safari

Horse Safari

Experience the serene beauty of Kusadası's countryside on a horse safari. Suitable for all levels of experience, this tour offers a unique way to connect with nature.

Horse Safari

Pamukkale

A UNESCO World Heritage Site, Pamukkale, also known as the Cotton Castle, is famous for its surreal white terraces filled with thermal waters. Nearby, you can also explore the ancient city of Hierapolis with its impressive Roman amphitheatre and well-preserved ruins.

Pamukkale

Sirince

Visit the quaint hilltop village of Sirince, renowned for its traditional houses, scenic beauty, and special tipples. Wander the narrow streets, visit local craft shops, and sample the village's famous fruit wines.

Each of these excursions provides a unique way to experience the rich culture, beautiful landscapes, and thrilling adventures that the region around Kusadası has to offer.

Sirince Village

5.2 Kuakmer Cultural Centre and Museum

Kuakmer Kusadası is a cultural centre and museum founded in 2014 by the Kusadası Municipality and the Kusadası Aegean Culture and Art Foundation (KEGEV). The centre is named after Fatma Ozel Arabul, a Turkish poet and writer who died in 2014.

Kuakmer Kusadası is located in the centre of Kusadası, about 200m from the Kusadası arch. The centre has a two-storey building with a total area of 1,500 square metres. The ground floor of the building houses the museum, while the first floor houses the cultural centre.

The museum has a collection of artefacts from the Roman, Byzantine, and Ottoman periods that showcase the history and culture of the town. A library and a research centre are also features of the museum.

The cultural centre hosts a variety of events, including art exhibitions, concerts, and theatre performances. The centre also offers a variety of educational programs, such as Turkish language courses and art classes.

Both tourists and locals enjoy visiting Kuakmer Kusadası. The centre is a great place to learn about the history and culture of Kusadası, and it also offers a variety of cultural and educational programs.

Here are some of the activities that you can do at Kuakmer Kusadası:

- Visit the museum and learn about the history and culture of Kusadası.
- Attend a concert or an art display.
- Watch a play or a dance performance.
- Take a Turkish language class or an art class.
- Attend a lecture or a workshop.
- Take a break on the terrace or garden.
- Enjoy a light meal at the cafe.

Kuakmer Kusadası is a great place to learn, create, and relax. It is a place where people from all over the world can come together to share their cultures and celebrate the arts.

CHAPTER 6
Kusadası History, Archaeological Sites, Beauty, and Vibrant Culture

6.1 The historical significance of Ephesus

Located a short distance from Kusadası, the ancient city of Ephesus, a UNESCO World Heritage Site, is a treasure trove for history enthusiasts, archaeologists, and lovers of antiquity. Once considered one of the most significant cities of the ancient world, Ephesus served as a prominent beacon of commerce, culture, and intellectual thought, with its influence spanning across centuries and civilisations.

In its prime, Ephesus was more than just a city; it was a thriving nexus of East and West, where diverse cultures intersected and flourished. Its streets were filled with merchants from distant lands, philosophers debating the mysteries of life, and artisans perfecting their craft. This energy, the spirit of Ephesus, left an indelible mark on the annals of history.

Playing a pivotal role during the Ionian, Roman, and Byzantine eras, Ephesus had a key role in shaping the socio-economic and political landscape of the region. Its strategic location near the Aegean Sea made it an important maritime trade centre, connecting the Mediterranean to Asia and beyond. The city's affluence was evident in its grand architecture and public spaces, which continue to impress visitors to this day.

Among the architectural marvels that stand testament to its past glory is the Agora, the city's main marketplace. Here, merchants from across the world would gather, their stalls brimming with exotic spices, fine silks, and handcrafted goods. The Agora was not just a centre for trade but also a social hub where news was exchanged and friendships were formed.

Then there's the grand amphitheatre, a spectacular venue that once resonated with the eloquent speeches of orators, the emotive performances of poets and musicians, and the enthusiastic cheers of spectators. As you stand in its midst, it's hard not to imagine the echoes of the past—the passionate debates, the theatrical performances, the roaring applause—all of which were a vital part of Ephesian life.

Ephesus, therefore, is not just an archaeological site; it's a fascinating window into the past. It offers a chance to walk in the footsteps of ancient Romans, to touch the stones they touched, and to experience the remnants of a civilisation that shaped the world as we know it today. The historical significance of Ephesus is a living testament to human ingenuity, resilience, and the unending quest for knowledge and progress.

6.2 A guided tour of Ephesus' highlights: Temple of Artemis, Library of Celsus, and others

Embarking on a guided tour of Ephesus is like journeying through time, each step revealing a new facet of the city's past. The ancient structures stand as silent witnesses to the city's rich history.

Library of Celsus: One of the most impressive structures is the Library of Celsus. This architectural treasure, once the third-largest library in the ancient world, served as a repository of knowledge and a monument to Roman Senator Tiberius Julius Celsus Polemaeanus, for whom it wasbuilt. The façade, with its meticulously carved details and two-storey Corinthian columns, still stops visitors in their tracks. Inside, the library once held as many as 12,000 scrolls, offering a wealth of knowledge to thecity's citizens. To walk through its remains today is to walk through the corridors of ancient wisdom.

Temple of Artemis: Equally remarkable is the Temple of Artemis, one of the Seven Wonders of the Ancient World. Once a magnificent edifice dedicated to the Greek goddess Artemis, the temple was an architectural marvel of its time. Although all that remains today is a single, solitary column, it continues to evoke a sense of awe and reverence, offering a poignant reminder of the temple's past glory. The vast site where the temple once stood, now surrounded by serene meadows, resonates with the echoes of past devotion and grand ceremonies.

Great Theatre: Another noteworthy highlight of Ephesus is the Great Theatre. With its capacity to accommodate 25,000 spectators, this imposing structure pays testament to the city's important cultural scene. The theatre, built into the hillside, was the venue for a variety of events, from dramatic performances and musical concerts to political gatherings and gladiatorial combats. The acoustics of the theatre were designed to carry even the softest whisper from the stage to the furthest seat, highlighting the architectural genius of the ancients. It was here that the citizens of Ephesus came together, not just to be entertained, but also to engage in public discourse, to be part of the collective decision-making process, and to partake in the cultural life of the city. The Great Theatre is not just an architectural wonder; it's a symbol of the democratic ethos of Ephesus, a place where every voice mattered and could be heard.

Each of these structures, from the Library of Celsus to the Temple of Artemis and the Great Theatre, tell tales of a city that was not just rich and powerful, but also a hub of intellectual and artistic pursuit. These enduring landmarks continue to inspire visitors who are able to imagine themselves as Ephesian citizens, if only for a day.

6.3 Tips and practical information for visiting Ephesus

When planning your visit to Ephesus, it's advisable to arrive early to beat the crowds and the heat. Wear comfortable walking shoes, as the site is expansive and the ground can be uneven. Don't forget to bring a hat, sun cream, and plenty of water.

Consider hiring a local guide or joining a guided tour to gain a deeper understanding of the site's history and significance. Lastly, remember to take your time and savour the experience—after all, walking through Ephesus is like stepping back in time, and that's a journey that deserves to be cherished.

6.4 The House of the Virgin Mary

Tucked away amidst the verdant foliage on the slopes of Bulbul Mountain, just a short distance from Kusadası, lies the House of the Virgin Mary. This humble stone dwelling, steeped in historical and religious significance, is believed by many to be the final earthly residence of the Virgin Mary, mother of Jesus Christ.

This serene sanctuary holds a shared significance for both Christians and Muslims, making it a unique testament to interfaith harmony. For Christians, it is a poignant reminder of Mary's crucial role in the story of Jesus, while Muslims revere Mary, or Maryam as she is known in Islam, as the mother of the prophet Isa (Jesus).

The house, with its modest architecture and peaceful surroundings, exudes a tranquil and reverential atmosphere that seems to transcend religious boundaries. Its simple, stone construction is a testament to the austere life Mary is believed to have led here, a stark contrast to the grandeur of many religious sites. Despite its simplicity, or perhaps because of it, the House of the Virgin Mary emanates an undeniable spiritual energy.

The site has evolved into a significant place of pilgrimage, attracting tens of thousands of visitors each year who come to pay their respects, to pray, or simply to soak in the peaceful ambience. Many visitors choose to drink from the sacred spring, which is believed to have healing properties, and to leave handwritten notes on the wall of wishes.

House of the Virgin Mary Wall of Wishes

The location of the house on Bulbul Mountain only adds to its appeal. The journey up the winding mountain road is a scenic delight, offering panoramic vistas of the surrounding olive groves, vineyards, and the shimmering Aegean Sea beyond.

Whether you are a person of faith seeking a deeper spiritual connection, a history enthusiast intrigued by the intertwining of religions, or a nature lover drawn to the idyllic setting, a visit to the House of the Virgin Mary promises to be a memorable experience, a moment of quiet reflection amidst the beauty of nature and the whispers of history.

6.5 Kervansaray

In the heart of Kusadası, a magnificent stone fortress stands as an enduring testament to the city's historical significance as a vital trading hub during the Ottoman Empire's golden age. Kervansaray, a splendid architectural feat of the 17th century, was erected under the auspices of the eminent Vizier Okuz Mehmet Pasha.

The Kervansaray, a concept rooted deeply in the Middle Eastern tradition of hospitality, served a multi-faceted purpose. It was an inn, a marketplace, and a sanctuary, all rolled into one. Travelling merchants, weary from long journeys along the ancient trade routes, found a haven within its solid walls. Here, they could rest and replenish, barter their goods in a secure environment, and tend to their pack animals.

Architecturally, Kervansaray is a fascinating spectacle. Its towering walls, built with locally sourced stone, guard the history within and reflect the defensive needs of the era. The intricately embellished gate, an elegant testament to the meticulous craftsmanship of the period, welcomes visitors into the central courtyard. This open area was the heart of the Kervansaray, a place for socialisation, negotiation, and camaraderie.

Kervansaray

Strategically located near the harbour, Kervansaray played a pivotal role in the commerce between the Mediterranean world and the Anatolian Peninsula (Asia Minor). It was more than just a building; it was a facilitator of cross-cultural interactions, as well as a melting pot of ideas and traditions.

In the present day, Kervansaray has undergone meticulous restoration to ensure its historical legacy is preserved. Its role has evolved with the passage of time. It no longer offers refuge to tired travellers or resonates with the lively bartering of merchants. Instead, it has been repurposed into a cultural hub, hosting an array of events that celebrate the city's arts scene.

Art exhibitions, musical performances, and cultural festivals now breathe new life into the historic structure. The enchanting central courtyard, bathed in the soft glow of evening lights, provides an atmospheric backdrop for these events. Visitors, both local and international, are drawn to the Kervansaray, not just to admire its architectural grandeur, but to immerse themselves in the multi-layered history and dynamic culture of Kusadası.

6.6 Pigeon Island: a picturesque fortress

A stone's throw away from the sun-kissed coast of Kusadası lies Pigeon Island, a small, enchanting isle connected to the mainland by a pedestrian causeway. As you make your way across the causeway, the gentle sea breeze and the sound of waves lapping at the shore create a serene and inviting atmosphere.

Pigeon Island is steeped in history, proudly housing the Byzantine- era fortress of Guvercinada Castle, which once played a crucial role as a strategic vantage point, safeguarding the harbour from the ever-present threat of pirate attacks. The island's name, in fact, derives from the word 'güvercin', meaning pigeon in Turkish, as these birds were used to send messages from the fortress.

Gsvercinada Or Pigeon Island

Today, visitors can wander among the fortress ruins, tracing the footsteps of the valiant guards who once patrolled these ancient walls. The island's well-maintained walking paths meander through lush gardens, adorned with colourful flowers and the soothing sounds of nature, providing a peaceful retreat from the hustle and bustle of modern life.

As you explore the island, be sure to take a moment to unwind at one of its quaint cafes. With the warm sun on your face, you can sip a refreshing beverage while marvelling at the panoramic vistas of Kusadası's stunning coastline. The shimmering blue waters, framed by the majestic mountains in the distance, paint a picture-perfect scene that is sure to capture your heart.

CHAPTER 7
Lesser-known Archaeological Sites Around Kusadası

While Ephesus is undoubtedly the crown jewel of archaeological sites in the Kusadası region, the surrounding area is also home to a wealth of lesser-known, yet equally appealing, historical treasures.

7.1 The ancient city of Priene: an architectural masterpiece

Priene: Hidden within the embrace of the Soke plain, under the watchful gaze of the craggy Mykale Mountain, lies the ancient Ionian city of Priene. This archaeological site, founded in the 8th century BCE, was once an energetic hub of activity and life.

Priene was a remarkable example of urban planning that was far ahead of its time. Its construction was based on a meticulously planned grid layout, an innovation attributed to the famous architect Hippodamus of Miletus. The city was carefully divided into rectangular blocks, with streets intersecting at right angles, a concept that would become a fundamental principle of urban planning in the future.

Priene

Today, the remnants of this once-thriving city, with its well- preserved ruins, offer a fascinating glimpse into the past. You can tread the same stone-paved streets that ancient Ionians once traversed, feel the imposing presence of the mighty Temple of Athena, and marvel at the remnants of civic buildings where important political decisions were made.

Priene

The city's private residences are a symbol of everyday life in ancient Priene. The ruins of the theatre, with its semi-circular seating arrangement and well-preserved stage building, evoke images of citizens gathered for performances and public assemblies.

But Priene is not just a trove of historical treasures; it also boasts an extraordinary natural setting. The city's strategic location offers panoramic views of the surrounding countryside and the serene Meander River winding its way through the fertile plain. Every turn in Priene brings with it a new vista, a blend of nature and antiquity that is both awe- inspiring and humbling. As the sun sets, painting the ancient stones in hues of gold and orange, the city seems to come alive, whispering tales of its glorious past to those who would listen.

Priene is a journey back in time, a must-visit for history enthusiasts eager to experience the past first-hand. At the same time, its natural beauty and tranquil ambience make it an ideal retreat for nature lovers seeking serenity and a break from the town. Whether you are a history buff, a nature enthusiast, or a curious traveller seeking off-the-beaten-path experiences, Priene promises an unforgettable encounter that you'll always remember.

7.2 The ancient city of Miletus

The ancient city of Miletus, steeped in history, traces its roots back to the Bronze Age, marking it as one of the oldest and most significant settlements in the region. As a prominent maritime city and a hub of intellectual pursuit, Miletus wielded considerable influence in the ancient world.

The city's expansive harbour, now silted up and replaced by tranquil marshland, was once the centre of the world of Miletus. It was a bustling place of trade and commerce, where merchant ships dropped anchor, laden with goods from across the Mediterranean. The harbour served as a vital connection point, bridging the city with distant lands, fostering cultural exchange, and ensuring its prosperity and prominence.

The modern visitor to Miletus is greeted by a landscape imprinted with the indelible marks of its illustrious past. The ruins of the city remain impressive and well worth a visit. The large theatre of Miletus, capable of accommodating 15,000 spectators, is an impressive sight to see.

Miletus

Equally fascinating is the city's Roman bath complex, an architectural marvel showcasing the advanced engineering skills of the ancient Romans. The baths, with their intricate mosaic floors, high arches, and the remains of hypocausts—an early form of heating system—offer a unique glimpse into the daily lives and recreational habits of the ancient Miletians. Here, citizens of all ranks would gather, not only to bathe and relax but also to socialize, conduct business, and engage in intellectual debates.

Miletus, with its rich historical legacy and beautifully preserved ruins, invites you to step back in time, to immerse yourself in its stories, and to experience the magic of a bygone era.

7.3 Didyma: Temple of Apollo

Not far from the lively streets of Kusadası lies the ancient city of Didyma. This city is home to the awe-inspiring ruins of the Temple of Apollo, a structure whose spiritual and architectural significance cannot be underestimated.

The Temple of Apollo was not merely a place of worship, but also home to one of the most important oracles in the ancient world. The temple was considered a powerful beacon of prophecy, attracting visitors from all corners of the world who sought divine guidance and insights into their fate. The oracle of Apollo at Didyma, known as the Didymaion, was second in importance only to Delphi in the ancient Greek world.

The city of Didyma itself was a hallowed site, a place imbued with profound spiritual energy and sanctity. It was here that the ancients would embark on their spiritual quest, traversing the sacred way from the city of Miletus to seek the wisdom of the oracle.

Temple of Apollo Didyma

Today, the Temple of Apollo stands as a marvel of Hellenistic architecture, its grandeur slightly faded but not forgotten. The temple's imposing columns, some of which still stand, reach skywards, evoking a sense of awe and reverence. The intricately carved reliefs on the surviving fragments of the temple provide a glimpse into the artistic prowess of the ancient sculptors. The vast sacred courtyard, although now open to the sky, continues to leave visitors awestruck.

Walking through these age-old ruins, one can't help but feel a profound connection to the past. The whispers of ancient prophecies seem to echo off the stone, and the impressive architectural feats of the Hellenistic period are all around. A visit to Didyma is not just an exploration of an ancient city; it's a journey into a world steeped in myth, religion, and architectural splendour.

7.4 The Basilica of St. John

Situated in the quaint town of Selcuk, just a short drive from Kusadası, lies the historic site of the Basilica of St. John. This sacred place, steeped in profound historical and religious significance, is traditionally believed to be the final resting place of John the Apostle, the author of the Fourth Gospel and the Book of Revelation.

John the Apostle, also known as St. John the Divine, was one of the twelve apostles of Jesus and is considered a significant figure in Christian tradition. His connection to the region adds a layer of deep spiritual resonance to the site, drawing both believers and history enthusiasts.

St John Basilica

The basilica itself, now standing in ruins, was once a grand and majestic edifice. Commissioned by Byzantine Emperor Justinian in the 6th century, it was designed in the shape of a cross and was lavishly decorated with beautiful mosaics, frescoes, and ornate stone carvings. In its heyday, the basilica was an important pilgrimage site. Devotees would journey from far and wide to pay their respects at the tomb of the revered apostle, seeking solace, inspiration, and spiritual enrichment.

Today, even in its ruined state, the Basilica of St. John exudes a quiet dignity and a real sense of history. The panoramic views of the surrounding countryside, including the imposing Ayasuluk Fortress and the tranquil Aegean Sea, make this place a must-visit. Whether you're a spiritual seeker, a lover of history, or simply a traveller in search of beautiful vistas, a visit to the Basilica of St. John promises a truly enriching experience.

7.5 Isa Bey Mosque

Also nestled in the heart of Selcuk is the Isa Bey Mosque. This remarkable building is a shining example of Seljuk architecture in Turkey, a testament to the artistic vision and architectural prowess of a bygone era. Constructed in the 14th century, the mosque is a blend of both Byzantine and Persian architectural influences.

The Isa Bey Mosque was commissioned by the Anatolian Seljuk Sultanate under the rule of Isa Bey, a member of the Aydinid dynasty. The mosque was not just a place of worship, but a complex that included a madrasa, or religious school, and a bathhouse, reflecting the holistic approach to communal life during the Seljuk period.

Isa Bey Mosque

The mosque's exterior is impressive, but it is within its hallowed interiors that the mosque truly reveals its splendour. Upon entering, one is immediately enveloped in a sense of tranquillity and reverence, enhanced by the soft light filtering through the windows and the intricate geometric and floral patterns adorning the walls.

One of the most striking features of the mosque is its stunning mihrab, a semicircular niche in the wall that indicates the direction of the Kaaba in Mecca. The mihrab is beautifully decorated with intricate carvings and calligraphy, displaying verses from the Qur'an. The grand arches and domes, adorned with elegant muqarnas—stalactite-like decorations—add to the mosque's architectural beauty.

The mosque's courtyard, with its ancient columns and ablution fountain, is an oasis of tranquillity. It offers a serene space for reflection and contemplation amidst the bustle of the modern world. The Isa Bey Mosque continues to invite visitors from around the world, providing a glimpse into the area's illustrious past and the timeless traditions of Islamic architecture and art.

Isa Bey Mosque

These lesser-known archaeological sites around Kusadası allow visitors to delve deeper into the region's rich past, making them a worthy addition to any traveller's itinerary.

CHAPTER 8
Natural Wonders: Exploring Kusadası's Breathtaking Landscapes

8.1 Dilek Peninsula National Park: flora, fauna, and outdoor activities

To the south of Kusadası, the Dilek Peninsula National Park is a protected sanctuary, showcasing an incredible array of ecosystems. From lush forests and thriving wetlands to rugged coastlines and unspoiled beaches, the park's incredible diversity beckons nature lovers and adventure seekers alike. Visitors are invited to traverse the park's numerous hiking trails, which meander gracefully through fragrant pine forests and offer beautiful views of the Aegean Sea.

Dilek Peninsula National Park

The park serves as a haven for an astonishing variety of flora and fauna, including wild boars, foxes, and a myriad of bird species that fill the air with their melodious songs. The thriving biodiversity that inhabits this protected area gives the park an environment of life and vibrancy.

Within the park's boundaries, beaches such as Icmeler Beach and Aydinlik Bay offer a tranquil refuge from the busier tourist spots. Whether you prefer to swim, sunbathe, or enjoy a peaceful picnic with friends and family, these beaches have something for everyone.

Dilek Peninsula National Park

Embrace the enchanting beauty and diversity of the Dilek Peninsula National Park, where nature's splendour unfolds before your eyes. This enchanted place promises to satisfy, whether you're looking for adventure, peace, or simply the chance to reconnect with nature.

8.2 Zeus Cave: an enigmatic underground treasure

Concealed amidst the rolling hills of the Dilek Peninsula, the enigmatic Zeus Cave beckons visitors to its entrance. This hidden subterranean chamber, filled with glistening, clear water, is steeped in local legend. It is said that the cave was once the clandestine bathing retreat for the mighty Greek god Zeus himself, offering him respite from the world above and the chance to revel in the serenity of this secret sanctuary.

Zeus Cave

To reach this mystical destination, visitors embark on a brief but invigorating hike, immersing themselves in the lush surroundings as they journey toward the cave. The anticipation builds with each step, as the promise of an extraordinary experience draws nearer.

Upon entering the cave, visitors are greeted with the refreshing embrace of its cool waters, inviting them to take a rejuvenating dip just as Zeus may have done. As they swim, the striking rock formations and the enchanting interplay of light and shadow create a mesmerizing tableau, emphasising the cave's natural beauty.

The Zeus Cave offers a rare opportunity to forge a connection with the myths and legends of a bygone era while revelling in the magnificence of the natural world. Whether you come seeking adventure or tranquillity, the experience of immersing yourself in the cave's pristine waters will linger long after you have returned to the world above.

8.3 Sirince Village: a hillside oasis

High in the hills above Selcuk, the enchanting village of Şirince provides a serene escape from the bustle of Kusadası's lively streets. This small, picturesque hamlet is renowned for its traditional stone houses, each of which exudes an air of rustic charm. The narrow cobblestone streets weave through the village, inviting you to discover the many treasures that Şirince has to offer.

As you stroll through this idyllic haven, you'll be captivated by the lush vineyards that blanket the hillsides, their vines heavy with the promise of a bountiful harvest. The village is famed for its locally-produced fruit wines, and visitors are encouraged to sample these delicious drinks, each sip a testament to the skill and passion of the local winemakers. The delicate bouquet and rich flavours are sure to delight your senses and awaken your appreciation for the art of winemaking.

Şirince Wines

In addition to its fruity offerings, Sirince is a place full of artisanal wonders. The village's charming shops are brimming with handcrafted goods, from intricately woven textiles to exquisite pottery, each piece created by the skilled artisans who live in the village.

Above all, Sirince is a place of repose and reflection, where you can pause and drink in the views of the surrounding countryside. The verdant hills roll into the distance, a soothing balm for the soul.

Let yourself be enchanted by the captivating village of Şirince, where tranquillity, charm, and natural splendour intertwine to create a haven in the hills that you will never forget.

8.4 Bafa Lake: a tranquil retreat

Enveloped by the majestic Latmos Mountains and the Aegean coastline, Bafa Lake is a tranquil and picturesque oasis, surrounded by olive groves and quaint fishing hamlets. Once an integral part of the Aegean Sea, the passage of time and the relentless accumulation of sediment deposits have transformed this bay into a serene and isolated haven, fostering a unique ecosystem that thrives with birdlife, such as pelicans and herons.

Bafa Lake

Visitors are invited to immerse themselves in all of the experiences that Bafa Lake has to offer, including boat tours, fishing excursions, and invigorating hikes. Each activity offers a memorable encounter with the natural splendour of this enchanting lake. All of them are sure to float your boat!

For those with a penchant for history and a thirst for discovery, the nearby ancient ruins of Heraclea beckon. Further afield, the Besparmak Mountains conceal rock-carved monasteries amidst their craggy peaks. These remarkable sanctuaries offer a glimpse into the lives of those who sought solace and spirituality within the embrace of the mountains.

Embark on a journey to Bafa Lake, where the enchanting fusion of nature, history, and serenity awaits.

8.5 Soke Plains: a patchwork of agricultural landscapes

The abundant Soke Plains, stretching to the north of Kusadası, stand as a living monument to the region's rich agricultural legacy. This vast, undulating expanse of land, with its endless patchwork of fertile fields, is adorned with flourishing cotton, wheat, and olive groves. For centuries, these agricultural treasures have served as the lifeblood of the region's economy and culture, shaping the lives of those who dwell within its embrace.

Visitors to this green paradise can immerse themselves in the authentic rural experience that the Soke Plains offers. Guided tours of local farms provide a fascinating insight into the daily lives and age-old traditions of the region's farmers, who have honed their skills and expertise season-by-season.

The Soke Plains are also home to numerous olive oil mills, where the region's prized olives are transformed into liquid gold. A visit to these mills offers a chance to explore the time-honoured techniques of olive oil production, from harvesting the fruit to the final pressing, as well as the chance to sample the fruits of these labours—the rich, fragrant oil that has become synonymous with the Mediterranean way of life.

At the heart of the Soke Plains lies Soke Market, a weekly bazaar that is the epicentre of local commerce and community. Here, farmers proudly display their freshly harvested produce and a dazzling array of handmade goods, their stalls overflowing with colour, texture, and enticing aromas.

The Soke Plains, with their combination of agricultural splendour, captivating traditions, and warm, welcoming community, offer an authentic glimpse into the heart and soul of this enchanting region. To visit these fertile lands is to forge a connection with the beauty of the earth and the generations of farmers who have nurtured its bounty.

Soke Cotton Fields

CHAPTER 9
A Tapestry of Cultures: The People and Traditions of Kusadası

9.1 The melting pot of Kusadası: a blend of ethnic and cultural backgrounds

Kusadası is much more than a picturesque coastal town adorned with stone and sand. It is an energetic place of diverse cultures and ethnicities, all of which come together in one beautiful melting pot. This diversity isn't a recent phenomenon but the product of an interwoven, centuries-old history.

The city has been a welcoming beacon to numerous civilisations over the ages. The Greeks, Romans, Byzantines, Seljuks, and Ottomans all have left their footprints on the sands of Kusadası, their influences seeping into the city's social, cultural, and architectural fabric. Each of these cultures, with their unique traditions, customs, and perspectives, has contributed to the city's cosmopolitan character, shaping its identity and spirit.

In the bustling markets, one can hear the echoes of the past, where Greek banter, Roman debates, Byzantine chatter, Seljuk discussions, and Ottoman tales once filled the air. The architecture, too, tells a story of convergence, where the Roman arches, Byzantine domes, Seljuk minarets, and Ottoman hamams blend seamlessly into the cityscape, creating a fascinating panorama of historical styles.

Modern Kusadası, while embracing the future, continues to celebrate this rich legacy. Its population is diverse, a testament to the city's tradition of acceptance and integration. This diversity manifests in the daily life of the city, in the food, the music, the festivals, and the languages spoken. It's a place where ancient traditions are not merely preserved but continue to thrive, coexisting harmoniously with modern sensibilities and global influences.

The city, like a seasoned storyteller, narrates a captivating tale of unity in diversity, a tale where different threads of ethnicities and cultures come together, weaving a story that is uniquely, undeniably Kuşadası. It's a place where the past and present, the local and global, the traditional and contemporary, all come together, creating an unforgettable cultural melody.

9.2 Traditional customs and important celebrations

One of the most enticing aspects of Kusadası's cultural richness lies in its traditional customs and practices. From momentous life events to annual holidays, these customs offer an engaging glimpse into the community's collective soul.

Weddings

Weddings in Kusadası are more than mere ceremonies; they are festivals brimming with joy and merriment, encapsulating the region's unbridled zest for life. They are grand spectacles that bring together family, friends, and community, creating an atmosphere that is electric with anticipation, excitement, and a sense of shared joy.

The festivities often kick off with the ritual of the henna night, an age-old tradition that sets the stage for the upcoming nuptials. On this special evening, the home of the bride-to-be is transformed into a hub of activity. The bride, the centre of attention, is adorned with intricate henna patterns on her hands and feet, symbolising fertility, love, and protection. These designs, carefully applied by a skilled artist, are not only beautiful to look at but also steeped in symbolic meaning.

As the henna dries, the women gather around the bride, their voices rising in the enchanting melodies of traditional songs. These songs, passed down through generations, tell stories of love, marriage, and life's many joys and challenges. As the women sing, they also share stories and impart words of wisdom to the bride, a poignant moment that highlights the community's close-knit bonds and shared heritage.

When the wedding day arrives, it is a lavish affair that reflects the city's love for grand celebrations. Family and friends from near and far gather for an delicious, elaborate feast, featuring a spread of traditional Turkish dishes. The air buzzes with lively conversation, laughter, and the clinking of glasses, as the attendees indulge in the feast and make merry.

Music is an integral part of the celebration, with traditional musicians setting the tempo for the festivities. The beats of drums and the melodies of traditional instruments fill the air, inviting everyone to the dance floor. As the bride and groom lead the dance, the guests join in, their movements expressing their joy and shared happiness.

Credit: Berkant Akbacak

Weddings in Kusadası are grand communal celebrations that embody love, unity, and a deep-rooted sense of cultural pride. If you get the chance to attend, you are guaranteed a wonderful time!

Sünnet

Circumcision, or 'sunnet' as it's known in Turkey, is an important religious and cultural tradition. As a majority-Muslim country, circumcision is a rite of passage for boys in Turkey, typically carried out when the child is between the ages of 5 and 12.

In Kusadası, as in many parts of Turkey, the sünnet celebration is a significant event that often involves the entire community. It's a time of joy and festivity, often as grand as a wedding, and is seen as a crucial step in a boy's journey to manhood.

Preparation for the sünnet ceremony can begin weeks, even months, in advance. The family of the boy being circumcised will send out invitations to relatives, friends, and neighbours, often expecting a large turnout. In the lead-up to the main event, the boy is often dressed in a special outfit, complete with a velvet cape and a king's crown, signifying his passage into adulthood.

On the day of the sünnet ceremony, the boy is paraded around the town in a decorated car or on horseback, usually accompanied by a procession of family and friends. Music, dancing, and sometimes even fireworks add to the celebratory atmosphere. Gifts are given to the boy, often in the form of gold coins or jewellery.

Credit: Berkant Akbacak

After the procession, a feast is held, complete with traditional Turkish food and sweets. It's a time for the community to come together, celebrating not just the boy's passage into manhood, but also their shared cultural and religious identity.

While the actual circumcision procedure is usually performed by a trained medical professional in a private setting, the social celebration surrounding the sünnet ceremony is a testament to the importance of this tradition in Kusadası and throughout Turkey.

Victory Day (30 August)

Kusadası, a city known for its warm and welcoming ambiance, truly embraces its festive spirit when it comes to the observance of national holidays and religious celebrations. Among these, Victory Day is a particular highlight, a national holiday that commemorates the triumphant conclusion of the Turkish War of Independence.

On this day, the city of Kusadası is transformed into a sea of red and white, the colours of the Turkish flag. Countless flags are hung from balconies, billow from poles, and are carried through the streets by locals and visitors alike, creating a strong display of national pride. The city's public spaces, historic landmarks, and residential areas are all adorned with these patriotic symbols, turning Kusadası into a living canvas that tells a story of national resilience and triumph.

Credit: Berkant Akbacak

The air in Kusadası is charged with excitement and patriotism, and it resonates with the sounds of the day's festivities. Parades fill the streets, featuring marching bands, local community groups, and representatives from the military and police forces. The rhythmic beats of drums, the tunes of traditional Turkish songs, and the cheers of the crowd create a symphony of sound that captures the spirit of Victory Day.

Speeches are another highlight of the day's observances. Local officials, community leaders, and sometimes ordinary citizens take to the stage to deliver speeches that pay tribute to the country's past struggles, celebrate its hard-won independence, and inspire a sense of unity and shared identity. These speeches serve as a reminder of the historical significance of Victory Day, and of the sacrifices that were made in the pursuit of freedom.

Credit: Berkant Akbacak

As the day draws to a close, the celebrations continue with concerts, fireworks displays, and communal feasts. The city's parks, squares, and seaside promenades become venues for these joyous gatherings, where locals and visitors can enjoy traditional Turkish cuisine, listen to live music, and witness spectacular fireworks in the sky.

Victory Day in Kusadası is more than just a day off from work or a break from routine. It is a celebration of national pride, a testament to the resilience of the Turkish people, and a shared moment of joy and unity for the city's inhabitants. Each year, as the city comes alive with patriotic ervour, it's clear that the spirit of Victory Day is deeply woven into the cultural fabric of Kusadası.

Religious Holidays

Religious holidays in Kusadası hold a special place in the hearts of the city's residents, offering a unique blend of spiritual reflection, communal unity, and festive celebration. As a city with deep roots in the Islamic tradition, the Islamic calendar dictates the rhythm of Kusadası's religious festivities, with each holiday adding something unique.

Kusadası experiences intense spiritual reflection and a time of strong community ties during the holy month of Ramadan. As the sun sets, the city comes alive with the spirit of 'Iftar', the meal that breaks the day's fast. Families and friends gather to share a meal, and the air is filled with the aroma of traditional Turkish dishes. The communal prayers at the local mosques, the festive atmosphere at the Iftar tents set up around the city, and the increased charity activities are all part of the Ramadan experience in Kusadası.

The end of Ramadan is marked by Eid al-Fitr, a three-day celebration often referred to as the 'Festival of Breaking the Fast'. The city is adorned with decorations, and the air resonates with the joyous sounds of celebrations. It's a time for prayer, feasting, and giving, with people visiting mosques for communal prayer, sharing meals with family and friends, and giving gifts and charity to those in need.

Eid al-Adha, also known as the 'Festival of Sacrifice', is another significant religious holiday in Kusadası. It commemorates the willingness of Ibrahim (Abraham) to sacrifice his son as an act of obedience to God. To mark this occasion, some families sacrifice an animal, usually a sheep or a goat, and distribute the meat to the poor, their neighbours, and within their own households.

Credit: Berkant Akbacak

Mevlid Kandili, the observance of the birth of Prophet Muhammad, is another important religious occasion in Kusadası. This is a time for prayer, reflection, and gratitude, with special services held in mosques, and families coming together to share meals and recite poetry and passages from the life of Prophet Muhammad.

In Kusadası, these religious holidays are not just about spiritual observance but are also an integral part of the city's social life. They bring the community closer, fostering a sense of unity, shared values, and mutual respect.

These traditional customs and rituals, whether they mark personal milestones or communal celebrations, act as the threads that weave the Kusadası community together. They reflect the shared values, the collective spirit, and the enduring cultural heritage of the city. Through these rituals, Kusadası's residents keep their history alive, passing down their cultural legacy from one generation to the next.

9.3 The role of religion and spirituality in Kusadası society

Religion and spirituality in Kusadası are a key part of the city's culture and identity. From the daily routines of its citizens to its grandest celebrations, from its architectural landscape to its communal practices, Kuşadası pulses with an undercurrent of faith that binds its people together, shaping their experiences and enriching their lives.

Kusadası's skyline is punctuated by the slender minarets of mosques reaching upward, casting a distinctive silhouette against thebackdrop of the setting sun. Five times a day, the muezzin's call to prayer reverberates through the city's streets, a rhythmic marker of time, guiding the daily life of its Muslim inhabitants. The Islamic calendar, with its cycle of fasting, feasting, and festivals, adds a unique cadence to the city's social life. The observance of Ramadan, with its communal iftars and nightly prayers, fosters a sense of community, while the joyous celebrations of Eid bring families together in a spirit of gratitude and generosity.

However, Kusadası's religious landscape also includes a significant Christian and Jewish heritage, which can be seen in its ancient churches and synagogues.

Church of St. Nicholas Near Priene

These places of worship stand as poignant reminders of a past where different faiths coexisted, each contributing to the city's cultural and spiritual identity. The Basilica of St. John, while no longer as vibrant as they once were, remain a testament to Kusadası's capacity to embrace diversity.

In Kusadası, religion extends beyond the realm of personal faith; it is a social and cultural phenomenon that fosters unity, promotes tolerance, and shapes collective consciousness. The city's religious practices, from the communal prayer at the mosque to the quiet contemplation at a church or synagogue, are not just rituals; they are shared experiences that bind its people together, transcending differences and fostering a sense of community. In these moments of shared spirituality, Kusadası emerges as a living, breathing community, where all faiths are recognised and valued.

9.4 Contemporary culture: music, art, and fashion influences

Although it boasts ancient ruins and traditional customs, Kusadası is also modern city with a thriving contemporary culture. The present-day cultural landscape of Kusadası is a dynamic amalgamation of the old and the new, the traditional and the innovative, the then and the now.

The city's music scene embodies this fusion. Traditional Turkish melodies, with their evocative rhythms and soulful lyrics, resonate in the city's music halls and cafes, preserving a connection with the region's rich musical heritage. Yet, these traditional sounds harmoniously coexist with contemporary genres. Pop, rock, and electronic music, influenced by western styles yet imbued with a distinctly Turkish flavour, echo from the city's nightclubs and music festivals.

Art is another realm where Kusadası's contemporary culture comes alive. Galleries showcasing the work of local and international artists are testament to the city's art scene. But art in Kusadası is not confined to these formal spaces. It spills out onto the streets, transforming the city into an open-air gallery. Murals brighten walls with their colourful narratives, and impromptu street performances add an element of spontaneity to the city's artistic expression. Sculptures and installations dot public spaces, each piece telling a story, sparking conversations, and reflecting the creative spirit of the city.

Fashion in Kusadası is an eclectic blend of traditional and modern styles. The city's fashion scene is a visual feast of bright colours, intricate patterns, and innovative designs. Traditional Turkish textiles, with their vivid hues and detailed embroidery, are a common sight, and these traditional elements are often seamlessly integrated with contemporary styles. Western trends influence the city's fashion, but they are adapted and reimagined through a uniquely Kusadası lens. This fusion of styles creates a fashion scene that is both familiar and fresh, traditional yet forward- looking.

Kusadası's contemporary culture, with its energetic music, thriving art, and eclectic fashion, reflects the city's ability to respect and preserve its past while embracing the new and the innovative.

CHAPTER 10
Artisanal Kuşadası: A Showcase of Local Crafts and Creations

Kusadası is a city that boasts an impressive array of traditional crafts and artisanal creations. Rooted in age-old techniques and passed down through generations, these crafts not only reflect the city's artistic heritage but also offer a unique way to connect with its culture and people.

10.1 The art of pottery and ceramics: traditional techniques and motifs

In Kusadası, the legacy of pottery and ceramics stretches back to the city's earliest civilisations. This art form, steeped in history and tradition, is an enduring symbol of the city's cultural richness and artisanal heritage.

Local artisans, the custodians of this time-honoured craft, skilfully shape the native clay into an array of forms: from elegant vases that echo the city's natural splendour, to ornate plates and tiles that find their place in everyday life. Each piece, a canvas in itself, is brought to life by the artist's touch. The artisans, wielding their brushes with the precision born out of years of practice, paint each piece by hand, infusing them with vibrancy and originality.

Traditional motifs, such as the tulip, the pomegranate, and the peacock, adorn the pottery and ceramic surfaces, creating a kaleidoscope of colours and intricate patterns. These motifs, rooted in the city's folklore and mythology, often tell tales of love, prosperity, and protection. For instance, the tulip symbolizes love and desire; the pomegranate, with its abundant seeds, represents fertility and prosperity; and the peacock, known for its beauty, is a symbol of immortality and spiritual awakening.

So, whether you're admiring the delicate beauty of a hand-painted tile, marvelling at the intricate patterns adorning a ceramic vase, or appreciating the skilled craftsmanship of a beautifully glazed plate, you're not just beholding a piece of art—you're experiencing a part of Kusadası's living history. The city's pottery and ceramics do not merely reflect its artistic heritage, they also offer a fascinating glimpse into its heart and soul.

10.2 Textiles and weaving: carpets, kilims, and traditional clothing

The rhythmic clacking of the loom is a familiar melody in the heart of Kusadası. It's the sound of the city's textile industry that thrives on age- old skills, passed down through generations. The city, renowned far and wide for its handwoven textiles, invites you to step into a world where every thread tells a tale, and every weave is a testament to the city's artistic prowess.

A quintessential symbol of this craftsmanship is the handwoven carpets and kilims of Kusadası. Each carpet, each kilim, is a labour of love and patience, requiring weeks, if not months, of meticulous work. Local weavers, masters of their craft, sit at their looms, their skilled fingers deftly manipulating the warp and weft. They weave intricate patterns and designs that come to life under their touch, blending vivid hues and a multitude of textures to create stunning pieces of functional art.

Credit: Berkant Akbacak

The motifs and patterns adorning these carpets and kilims are more than just decorative elements. They are visual stories, symbols that narrate tales of cultural heritage, local folklore, and personal experiences. From the 'Eye' motif, believed to ward off evil, to the 'Hands on Hips' symbol, representing female fertility and motherhood, each pattern carries a depth of meaning that goes beyond its aesthetic appeal.

Equally captivating is the traditional clothing of Kusadası, a reflection of the city's rich cultural heritage and its people's lifestyle. From the flowing 'shalvar' trousers, an embodiment of comfort and elegance, to the hand-embroidered 'yelek' vests, resplendent in their bright colours and intricate motifs, each piece is a blend of practicality and beauty.

94

The shalvar, with its loose fit and lightweight fabric, is designed for comfort in the warm Mediterranean climate, while the yelek, embellished with delicate embroidery and beads, adds a touch of glamour to the ensemble. Other traditional items include the 'turban', a piece of fabric worn on the head that serves both a functional and a ceremonial purpose, and the 'kaftan', a long robe-like garment which dates back thousands of years.

These traditional garments, like the carpets and kilims, bear the mark of Kusadası's skilled artisans. Each stitch, each thread, is a testament to their passion and dedication, transforming ordinary fabrics into exquisite pieces of wearable art. As such, the textiles and garments of Kusadası are not just products, but cherished mementos of a city that weaves its culture into every thread, every weave, and every stitch.

Carpets and Kilims

10.3 Jewellery and metalwork: intricate designs and skilled craftsmanship

In the bustling bazaars and tranquil workshops of Kusadası, the mellow glow of gold, the shimmer of silver, and the lustre of bronze come alive under the experienced hands of local jewellers and metalworkers. Here, the ancient craft of jewellery and metalwork, a cornerstone of the city's artisanal heritage, thrives amidst the harmonious cacophony of hammers striking metal, chisels sculpting intricate designs, and polishers bringing out the brilliant shine of precious metals.

Kusadası's jewellers are true masters of their craft. With a discerning eye and a steady hand, they transform raw metals and gemstones into exquisite pieces of jewellery that will appeal to everyone. From delicate silver earrings that capture the playfulness of the Aegean waves, to ornate gold necklaces that echo the grandeur of Kusadası's rich history, each piece demonstrates their artistry and meticulous attention to detail.

These artisans often incorporate traditional motifs into their designs, adding a touch of cultural authenticity that sets their creations apart. The 'Evil Eye' motif is a common element in jewellery designs, as are floral motifs inspired by the natural beauty of the region. Some jewellers also specialize in reproducing designs from different eras of the city's history, creating pieces that offer a tangible connection to Kusadası's past.

Equally impressive is the craftsmanship of Kusadası's metalworkers. Using techniques that have been honed over centuries, these artisans shape, engrave, and emboss metal into a variety of objects, from functional utensils to decorative items. Bronze coffee pots, copper plates, and brass lanterns are just a few examples of their work, each piece reflecting the practical aesthetics and the artful elegance that define Kusadası's artisanal scene.

Whether you're admiring a masterfully crafted piece of jewellery or a finely wrought metal artefact, the city's craftsmanship leaves you in awe, reminding you of the creative energy that pulses through Kusadası's lanes, workshops, and markets. As such, the city's jewellery and metalwork do more than just adorn bodies or decorate spaces; they narrate tales of cultural pride, artistic passion, and a rich heritage that continues to inspire and thrive.

10.4 Markets and boutiques: shopping for unique souvenirs

Immersing yourself in Kusadası's artisanal culture extends beyond appreciating the city's crafts. It also involves stepping into the lively bazaars and charming boutiques that pepper the city, where the air is steeped in the rich aroma of spices, the colourful array of handicrafts vies for your attention, and the chorus of vendors haggling over prices fills the air.

These markets are the beating heart of Kusadası's artisanal scene, a veritable maze of stalls that overflow with the city's finest crafts. Row upon row of delicately painted ceramics catch the eye of tourists and art lovers alike. Handwoven carpets and kilims lie stacked high, their intricate patterns telling tales of tradition and history. Stalls lined with handcrafted jewellery sparkle under the soft glow of the overhead lanterns, each piece a testament to the city's talented jewellers.

In these busy marketplaces, shopping is more than a transaction; it's an experience, a journey into the soul of Kusadası's artisanal heritage. Each item you pick up, be it a beautifully crafted ceramic vase, a pair of silver earrings, or a handwoven carpet, has a story to tell—of the hands that shaped it, the traditions that inspired it, and the city that nurtured it.

For those looking for a more curated shopping experience, Kusadası's boutiques offer a carefully selected array of local crafts. Housed in charming storefronts, these boutiques present an intimate setting where you can take your time to appreciate the fine details of each creation, learn about its history, and even meet some of the artisans behind the works.

Whether you're on the hunt for a unique souvenir, a piece of home decor that carries the spirit of Kusadası, or a gift that encapsulates the city's artistic flair, these markets and boutiques are a must-visit. And as you haggle over prices in the traditional manner and exchange stories with the friendly vendors, you'll be supporting the local economy, preserving age- old crafts, and participating in a cultural tradition that is as old as Kusadası itself.

CHAPTER 11
Festivals and Celebrations: Kusadası's Lively Calendar of Events

Kusadası is a city that loves to celebrate. From religious observances and cultural festivals to art events and food celebrations, Kusadası's calendar is full of events that reflect both the city's diverse heritage and its contemporary scene. These festivities not only offer a joyous respite from the everyday but also serve to strengthen communal bonds and celebrate the city's unique identity.

11.1 Cultural and religious festivals: Hidirellez

Alongside Ramadan and Eid, Kusadası also celebrates Hidirellez (6 May), a traditional festival that marks the arrival of spring. The festival, celebrated with music, dancing, and feasting, blends Islamic traditions with pre-Islamic rituals associated with nature and fertility.

11.2 Music, art, and film events: Kusadası Jazz Festival and others

When it comes to celebrating the arts, Kusadası pulls out all the stops. A robust calendar of music, art, and film events, scattered throughout the year, are a testament to the city's artistic vitality, offering both residents and visitors an opportunity to immerse themselves in a creative ambiance that is inimitably Kusadası.

Among the numerous festivals that the city hosts, the Kusadası Jazz Festival is a highlight. This prestigious event is not just a celebration of jazz music but a cultural gathering that transcends borders. Each year, the festival draws a lineup of impressive talent, featuring both acclaimed international artists and rising stars from the local jazz scene. The city's atmospheric venues, ranging from intimate jazz clubs to open-air stages, are filled with the soulful, improvisational strains of jazz music. Audiences can enjoy a variety of performances that explore the diverse facets of jazz, from its roots in African-American communities to its global contemporary iterations. The Kusadası Jazz Festival is a truly immersive experience.

Along with its thriving music scene, Kusadası also nurtures cinematic talent through its annual film festival. This event provides a platform for film makers, both seasoned and novice, to showcase their work to a discerning audience. The festival features a broad spectrum of films, from local independent productions to internationally acclaimed features, fostering dialogue between different cinematic traditions and narratives. Panel discussions, workshops, and Q&A sessions with the film makers further enrich the festival experience, encouraging a deeper understanding of the art of film making. The Kusadası Film Festival not only celebrates the magic of cinema but also contributes to the growth of a dynamic cinematic culture in the city.

11.3 Food and wine celebrations: Olive Harvest Festival and vineyard tours

Kusadası hosts a number of food and wine events, most notably the Olive Harvest Festival. This festival marks the end of the olive harvest with communal feasts, folk dances, and local crafts, celebrating the importance of the olive tree in the region's agriculture and cuisine.

Wine lovers can also join in the festivities with vineyard tours that showcase the region's winemaking traditions. These tours offer a glimpse into the process of winemaking, from grape to glass, and often culminate in wine tastings that celebrate the rich flavours of the region's wines.

11.4 Sports events and competitions

In addition to its cultural and historical offerings, Kusadası also hosts a variety of annual sports events and competitions that cater to diverse interests, from sailing to running and more.

Blessed with a prime location on the Aegean Sea, Kusadası naturally lends itself to a host of water sports. Among these, sailing stands out as a favourite. The art and sport of sailing are celebrated annually in the much-anticipated Kusadası Sailing Regatta, an event that transforms the city's serene waters into a thrilling arena of competition and camaraderie.

The Kusadası Sailing Regatta is more than just a sporting event; it's a global gathering that brings together sailing enthusiasts from every corner of the world. Experienced sailors, budding amateurs, and passionate spectators descend on the city to partake in or witness this exciting spectacle. The regatta's schedule is packed with a series of races, testing the participants' sailing prowess as they navigate their vessels through the waters of the Aegean, guided by the wind and their own strategic expertise.

One of the most captivating sights of the regatta is the panorama of colourful sails billowing against the clear blue sky, their hues mirrored in the shimmering waters below. This is not just a feast for the eyes but a testament to the spirit of the event and the sport itself—a blend of competition, skill, and a shared love for the sea.

Beyond the thrill of the races, the Kusadası Sailing Regatta also presents an opportunity for cultural exchange and socialising. Sailors and spectators alike gather to share stories, learn from one another, and celebrate their shared passion for sailing. Evenings are filled with lively events, from award ceremonies to beachside parties, all set against the backdrop of the setting sun.

Kusadası also hosts several running events throughout the year. The Kusadası Half Marathon is a popular event that brings together professional runners, amateur athletes, and fitness enthusiasts for a challenging race along the city's scenic routes. The event also includes shorter races and fun runs, making it a family-friendly event that promotes health and fitness.

For those who enjoy team sports, the Kusadası Football Tournament is a highlight. This competition sees local clubs and teams from around the region battle it out on the pitch, drawing large crowds of passionate football fans. The tournament is celebrated not just for the sporting action on the field, but also for the camaraderie and sportsmanship that it fosters among the teams and their supporters.

The city's sports calendar also includes events like beach volleyball tournaments, windsurfing competitions, and cycling races, ensuring that there's something for every sports enthusiast.

11.5 Camel wrestling in Kusadası: a unique tradition

Camel wrestling is a deeply-rooted tradition in many parts of Turkey, and Kusadası is no exception. This annual event, generally held during the winter months, is a spectacle that draws locals and tourists alike.

Camel wrestling in Kusadası is more than just a sport; it's a cultural festival, a social event, and a celebration of a long-held tradition. On the day of the event, you'll find the town buzzing with excitement and anticipation. The festivities begin early in the morning, with the camels, adorned with colourful, ornate saddles, parading through the streets, accompanied by musicians and enthusiastic onlookers.

The wrestling event itself involves two male camels, generally goaded on by a female camel in heat. The male camels wrestle each other by using their necks as leverage, aiming to make their opponent fall or retreat. The sight of these powerful beasts locked in a test of strength is truly a sight to behold. However, it's important to note that the camels are not harmed during these events, and any sign of distress from a camel ends
the match immediately.

Credit: Berkant Akbacak

Aside from the wrestling, the event is also a chance for locals to socialise and celebrate. The air is filled with the aroma of traditional Turkish foods being cooked at nearby stalls, and the sounds of folk music and laughter create a festive atmosphere. Handcrafted goods, from camel-themed souvenirs to traditional Turkish crafts, are also on sale during the event.

While camel wrestling may not be a common sight in many parts of the world, it is a cherished tradition in Kusadası. Attending a camel wrestling event offers a unique glimpse into the local culture and an opportunity to experience a tradition that has been passed down through generations. Whether you're a sports enthusiast, a culture buff, or simply a curious traveller, witnessing a camel wrestling event in Kusadası should be on your bucket list.

CHAPTER 12
Shop Till You Drop: Kusadası's Markets and Shopping Destinations

12.1 Kusadası's weekly bazaar: a feast for the senses

Every Tuesday, Wednesday, and Friday, Kusadası transforms into a hub of activity as its weekly bazaar takes over the heart of the city. This busy open-air market, conveniently located near the town centre, is a sensory feast and a celebration of local life that unfolds amidst a colourful display of stalls, chattering vendors, and curious shoppers.

The bazaar is the place to come for fresh produce. As you navigate through the labyrinthine lanes, you'll find an abundance of locally-grown fruits and vegetables, each pile a riot of colour, from the fiery red of ripe tomatoes to the sunny yellow of fresh lemons. The rich, mouthwatering aroma of ripe peaches mingles with the earthy scent of fresh herbs, and every corner of the market brims with the promise of a delicious meal waiting to be cooked.

But the bazaar isn't just a paradise for fruit and vegetables. It also boasts an impressive array of aromatic spices that transport you to the heart of Turkish cuisine. Piles of red paprika, golden turmeric, and a myriad of other spices greet visitors, their intoxicating scent filling the air. Nearby, you'll find stalls selling lokum (Turkish delight) in every flavour and colour.

Apart from the culinary delights, on Wednesdays the bazaar is also a great place to find textiles, clothing, and accessories. Look out for brightly coloured fabrics, intricate lacework, traditional Turkish carpets, and hand-embroidered things to wear.

The bazaar is also full of trinkets, ceramics, and souvenirs, making it an ideal place to shop for unique gifts and mementoes. Handmade jewellery, traditional pottery, and beautifully crafted leather goods offer a piece of Kusadası that you can take home with you.

12.2 The Grand Bazaar and Orient Bazaar

Kusadası's Grand Bazaar and Orient Bazaar are located near the harbour (Ege Port) and here visitors can find a huge array of goods. Among the most popular are high-quality leather items, which range from stylish jackets and durable boots to elegant purses and wallets. There are also handwoven carpets and gold and silver jewellery on offer. It's a shopper's paradise!

Beyond leather, carpets, and jewellery, the shops also offer traditional Turkish crafts. You'll find ornate ceramics painted in vivid colours, embroidered textiles that showcase the region's distinctive needlework techniques, and delicate glassware that glimmers in the sunlight.

As you navigate the shops, be prepared to engage in the time- honoured tradition of haggling. Bargaining is an integral part of the shopping experience here, and it's not uncommon for prices to be significantly marked down after a bit of friendly negotiation. The process is a dance of sorts, a back-and-forth exchange that adds a layer of excitement to the shopping experience. So, what are you waiting for? Step into these Bazaars of Kusadası and grab yourself a bargain!

12.3 Kusadası's Marina and Shopping Centre: modern retail therapy

For a more contemporary shopping experience, Kusadası's Marina and modern shopping centres offer a wide range of international and local brands, as well as dining and entertainment options. The upscale Kusadası Marina is home to stylish boutiques, designer stores, and trendy cafes, all set against the backdrop of luxury yachts floating on the Aegean Sea.

Shopping centres like the **Kusadası AVM** and **Novada Park** provide a convenient, air-conditioned environment for browsing popular fashion, electronics, and home goods retailers. Some of these shopping centres also feature cinemas, children's play areas, and a variety of restaurants and cafes, ensuring a fun day out for the whole family.

Kusadasi AVM

Novada Outlet

12.4 Discovering Kusadası's creative side: an exploration of local Art galleries and craft shops

Kusadası has long been a source of inspiration for both artists and artisans. Art galleries are scattered throughout Kusadası, providing a platform for local artists to showcase their talent. These spaces house a diverse collection of artworks, ranging from traditional oil paintings that depict the city's mesmerizing sunsets and busy bazaars, to contemporary sculptures that push the boundaries of form and function.

Ibramaki Art Gallery Kusadasi

Exhibition of local artists

Back row: Melek Ikiz, Zeynep Kaya, Nilufer Alper, Nadya Ates, Emel Cevikcan, Tatjana Breous, Yesim Gulseven, Ghazal Ghazemi Irani, Gulizar Kilic, Arya Kamalı, Mehmet Kırıckaya, Gülnur Çavus, Sevim Karaoglu, Sevim Kumova, Pinar Soyturk, Nursen Turhal Mengeş

Front row: Nilgun Vural, Hayal İrtıgün, Esen Eris Ercan, Nasrah Nefer, Serap Unveren, Irmak Persia Kamalı

A visit to these galleries is more than just a shopping experience. It's an opportunity to engage with the city's creative community, to understand their inspirations and artistic processes, and to appreciate the skill and passion that go into each piece. Art enthusiasts and collectors will find much to admire in these spaces, from the bold brushstrokes of a local painter's canvas to the delicate craftsmanship of a ceramicist's clay creations.

Whether you're an art aficionado or a curious traveller, these spaces provide a unique opportunity to explore Kusadası's artistic soul, to appreciate its crafts, and to connect with its creative community.

12.5 Tips for shopping in Kusadası: bargaining, currency, and souvenir ideas

When shopping in Kusadası, it's essential to keep a few tips in mind for a smooth and enjoyable experience. As stated, bargaining is expected, especially in markets and bazaars, so don't be afraid to negotiate for a better price. It's also a good idea to carry some Turkish lira, as not all vendors accept credit cards. When selecting souvenirs, consider purchasing items that can only be found in Kusadası, such as locally-produced olive oil, hand-painted ceramics, or traditional textiles.

Whether searching for unique souvenirs, local handicrafts, or the latest fashion trends, Kusadası offers a shopping experience to suit every taste and budget. Happy shopping!

CHAPTER 13
Savouring Kusadası: An In-depth Exploration of Dining and Nightlife

13.1 Dining in Kusadası: a culinary journey from humble lokantas to luxury Marina experiences

Kusadası offers a host of dining options that cater to every food lover's preference and budget. Drawing from Aegean, Mediterranean, and central Anatolian cuisines, Kusadası offers a delicious fusion of tastes and culinary styles. There really is something for everyone!

At the heart of the city's culinary culture are the local lokantas, traditional Turkish eateries that serve a variety of delectable, home-cooked meals. These establishments, often family-run, have an inviting, down-to-earth atmosphere, where both locals and tourists gather to enjoy hearty dishes. The menu at a lokanta usually features a buffet-style spread of beloved Turkish classics. From comforting 'manti' (Turkish dumplings), to savoury 'pide' (Turkish-style pizza), and an assortment of 'mezes' (appetizers), lokantas offer an authentic taste of Turkey's rich culinary heritage, all served with the ubiquitous—and tasty—Turkish tea.

As the day transitions into evening, the Kusadası Marina starts to buzz with life. This upscale district is home to a range of exquisite fine dining establishments. Here, culinary expertise and creativity combine to create beautifully crafted dishes, marrying traditional Turkish ingredients with modern, innovative culinary techniques. Dining in the Marina is not just about the food, but the whole experience, from the elegant settings and professional service to the mesmerizing views of yachts bobbing gently in the harbour under the starlit sky.

Marina Fine Dining

13.2 Nightlife in Kusadası: from energetic bars to vibrant nightclubs and traditional Turkish entertainment

Kusadası's nightlife, much like its dining scene, caters to a range of preferences. Whether you're in the mood for an intimate evening, an energetic night of dancing, or a cultural experience, you'll find what you're after in Kusadası.

Sadly, Kusadası Bar Street has changed significantly over time and not in a good way. It used to be a busy centre that attracted both locals and visitors. Sadly, what was once renowned for its vibrant ambiance, buzzing bars, and entertainment venues has come to be associated with a different kind of activity. The street, which was formerly a representation of social interaction and pleasure, has declined in a big way. The area's once vibrant energy has definitely diminished as a result of this change, overshadowing recollections of its glory days and leaving just a shell of its previous vibrant self.

With so many good bars and clubs along the seafront and in the Old Town (Kaleici) area my recommendation is to visit the Old Town area, you will not be disappointed!

For a more relaxed, culturally immersive evening, the Kaleici area, also known as Kusadası's old town, is a must-visit. This charming district, with its narrow, cobblestone streets and traditional stone houses, is home to disco clubs as well as cosy bars and restaurants that offer a more laid-back ambiance. Here, you can savour a leisurely meal accompanied by a glass of local wine or raki, the aniseed-flavored Turkish spirit. Kaleici also offers traditional Turkish entertainment, with live music performances and folk dances that will make you stop and stare. The sounds of traditional instruments, like the 'saz' or 'oud', waft through the air, adding to the enchanting atmosphere.

Credit: Berkant Akbacak

For those looking to dance the night away, Kusadası boasts several nightclubs where local and international DJs keep the music flowing until dawn. These venues offer a lively atmosphere, where you can lose yourself to the rhythm of the music and make unforgettable memories.

As you explore Kusadası's nightlife further, you'll find many establishments offering Turkish 'fasil' music, a genre associated with the nation's traditional taverns, known as 'meyhanes'. As you dine, musicians serenade you with this entrancing music, adding a unique, cultural twist to your dining experience

For an even deeper dive into Turkish culture, don't miss the opportunity to enjoy a traditional Turkish 'Sema' or whirling dervish performance. This mesmerising dance is not just a cultural spectacle but a form of moving meditation, reflecting the spiritual journey of the dancer. These performances, usually accompanied by 'ney' (a traditional Turkish flute) music and chanting, offer a unique experience that is deeply moving.

In addition, the old town of Kaleici hosts several festivals and events throughout the year that highlight local music, dance, and culinary traditions. These events transform the charming streets of the old town into cultural hubs, where you can learn more about Kusadası's heritage.

From casual lokantas serving hearty, traditional Turkish dishes to high-end restaurants at the marina offering refined culinary experiences, Kusadası's dining scene is as diverse as it is delicious. And when the sun sets, the city's nightlife comes alive, offering everything from energetic clubs and bars to traditional Turkish entertainment.

This blend of modern and traditional, local and global, creates a feeling that is uniquely Kusadası. So whether you're a foodie, a culture enthusiast, a party-goer, or all of the above, Kusadası has something to make your visit an unforgettable one.

CHAPTER 14
Practical Tips and Travel Information for Your Kusadası Adventure

14.1 Getting to Kusadası: air, land, and sea

Kusadası is easily accessible via various transportation options. The nearest airport, Izmir Adnan Menderes International Airport, is located about 70 kilometres north of the town and offers flights to and from major cities in Europe and Turkey. From the airport, visitors can take a shuttle bus, rent a car, or arrange for a private transfer to Kusadası.

Alternatively, Kusadası can be reached by bus from cities like Istanbul, Ankara, and Izmir, or by ferry from the Greek island of Samos during the summer months.

14.2 Accommodation options in Kusadası

Kusadası's accommodation caters to the needs of all types of travellers, whatever their budget and requirements. The city presents an impressive selection of places to stay, ranging from opulent resorts and charming boutique hotels to budget-friendly hostels and homely guesthouses, ensuring that every visitor can find a home away from home wherever they lay their head.

Luxury seekers will find what they are after in Kusadası's premium resorts and five-star hotels, which often grace the stunning beachfront or are strategically located near the city centre. These properties offer a lavish retreat, combining deluxe amenities such as private beaches, sparkling pools, spa facilities, and gourmet dining options, all wrapped in a package of exceptional service.

5 Star Resorts

Unique 5 Star Lifestyle

Boutique hotels, on the other hand, provide a more intimate and personalised experience. Often housed in beautifully restored buildings, these establishments boast a unique character and charm. Each room is typically designed with a keen eye for detail, offering a blend of local aesthetics and modern comforts. Some boutique hotels also feature on-site restaurants that serve local and international cuisine, providing guests with an authentic culinary experience without having to step out of their accommodation.

Boutique Hotels

Boutique Hotel

For travellers on a budget, Kusadası doesn't disappoint. The city is dotted with numerous hostels and budget hotels that offer comfortable and clean accommodation at an affordable price. These establishments often provide communal spaces, like lounges and kitchens, promoting a sense of community among travellers. And while they may be light on the wallet, they don't skimp on location. Many budget accommodations are conveniently situated near popular attractions or well-connected transport hubs, making it easy for guests to explore the city.

Budget Hotels

Budget Hotel

Guesthouses and bed-and-breakfast establishments, typically found in the quieter neighbourhoods and charming villages surrounding Kusadası, offer a homely and relaxed atmosphere. Here, guests can experience the warmth of Turkish hospitality, often with home-cooked meals and personalised service from the hosts.

Whether you're a luxury traveller seeking a plush seaside resort, a culture enthusiast looking for a charming boutique hotel, a budget-conscious backpacker in need of a friendly hostel, or a family seeking the warmth of a cosy guest house, Kusadası's wide array of accommodation options ensures you'll find the perfect place to stay after a day of adventure and exploration.

14.3 Local transportation: getting around Kusadası

Navigating Kusadası is a breeze, thanks to its compact nature and efficient public transportation system. While the town's size allows for many areas to be comfortably explored on foot, journeys that require covering longer distances are well-serviced by the local dolmuş system and a network of readily available taxis.

The Dolmus, a type of shared minibus that's an integral part of Turkish public transport, is a popular choice due to its affordability and convenience. These minibuses are marked with numbers 1 through 7, each representing a different route that winds through various parts of Kusadası and its surrounding attractions. Whether you're heading to the local market, a nearby beach, or an ancient historical site, there's a dolmuş that can get you there.

Currently, the dolmus system operates with a flat fare per trip, making it a cost-effective option for exploring the town. Although there are designated dolmuş stops, these minibuses are not restricted to specific bus stops. Instead, they operate on a more flexible system that's characteristic of Turkish hospitality. To hail a dolmuş, you simply have to stick out your hand, and the driver will pull over at the nearest safe location. Similarly, when you wish to disembark, simply inform the driver, and they will stop at the next suitable spot.

Dolmuş Routes 1-7

Dolmuş Number 1 Route

From Nato To Kustur: Nato Evleri-Sanayi Sitesi-Suleyman Demirel Blv.-Adnan Menderes Blv.-Candan Tarhan Blv.- Hasan Reis Blv.- Huseyin Reis Caddesi-Ataturk Blv.-İnonu Blv.- Adnan Menderes Blv.-Şevki Hasırcı Meydanından Candan Tarhan Bulvarına dönüş-Hasan Reis Bulvarı-Hülya Kocyigit Cd.-Gazi Beğendi Blv.- Eski Kusadası Selçuk Yolu— Turgut Ozal Blv.-Kustur Onu Yolu Caddesi- Ephesus Princes Otel (Last Stop) Kırmızı Hat

Dolmuş Routes 1-7

Dolmuş Number 1A Route

From Kustur To Nato: Ephesus Princes-Kustur Onü Yolu Cd.-Turgut Ozal Blv.-Eski Kusadası Selçuk Yolu-Gazi Begendi Blv..— Ataturlc Blv.-inönü Blv. - Adnan Menderes Blv.-Süleyman Demirel Blv-Sanayi Sitesi.-Nato Evleri

Dolmuş Routes 1-7
Dolmuş Number 2 Route

From University To Nural Kent: Ahmet Gundem Sitesi- 4.Sk.-Kusadası Devlet Hastanesi- Hulya Kocyigit Cd-Ataturk Bulvarı [. Sk.—Huseyin Reis Cd.— Enver Reis Sk.-Sacıkara Sk.—Gulhan Arın Blv.- Denizci Sk.- Çetin Emeç Cd.- Bahce Arası Sk.-İnönü Blv.- Sabri Mumcu Cd.- Şht. Usttegmen Cemalettin Yılmaz Cd.- Suleyman Demirel Blv.-Kemer Cd.- Yuksel Yalova Cd.- Kasım Yaman Cd.-507 Sokak— Nural kent Sitesi (Son Durak)

From Nural Kent To University: Nural kent Sitesi- 507 Sk.-Kasım Yaman Cd.—Yuksel Yalova Cd.-Kemer Cd.-Koctas Yolu-Altın Kaynak Cd. 6. Sk.- Şht. Usttegmen Cemalettin Yılmaz Cd- Otogar Kavsagından dönüş - Süleyman Demirel Blv.-Şht. Usttegmen Cemalettin Yılmaz Cd.- Sabri Mumcu Cd.—İnönü Blv.-Adnan Menderes Blv.-Şevki Hasırcı Meydanı-Candan Tarhan Blv.-Bahcearası Sk.— lnönü Blv. — 50. Yıl Cd.- Candan Tarhan Blv.- Gülhan Arın Blv- Sacıkara Sk- Enver Reis Sk- Hüseyin Reis Cd.-2. Sk.—4.Sk.-Hasan Reis Blv.—Hulya Koçyigit Cd.— Kusadası Devlet Hastanesi- Ahmet Gündem Sitesi- University

Dolmuş Routes 1-7

Dolmuş Number 2/10 Route

University To Notestik: Üniversite(Turizm İşletmeciliği ve Otelcilik Y.O.) - Ahmet Gündem Sitesi- 4.Sk.-Kuşadası Devlet Hastanesi- Hülya Koçyiğit Cd— Atattlrk Bulvarı [. Sk.-Hüseyin Reis Cd.- Enver Reis Sk.- Saçıkara Sk.-Gülhan Arın Blv.- Denizel Sk.—Çetin Emeç Cd.- Bahçe Arası Sk.-lnönü Blv.— Sabri Mumcu Cd.- Şht. Üstteğmen Cemalettin Yılmaz Cd.— Süleyman Demirel Blv.- Kemer Cd.- Altın Kaynak Caddesi 2. Sk.— Şht. Hava Pilot Yzb. Akgül Sezginer Sk.-Yüksel Yalova Cd.- Hüseyin Can Cd.-Notestik yolu- Notestik (Son Durak)

Notestik To University: Notestik-Notestik Yolu- Hüseyin Can Cd.- Yüksel Yalova Cd.- Şht. Hava Pilot Yzb. Akgül Sezginer Sk.- Koçtaş Yolu- AltınKaynak Cd. 6. Sk.- Şht. Üstteğmen Cemalettin Yılmaz Cd- Otogar Kavşağından dönüş - Süleyman Demirel Blv.-Şht. Üstteğmen Cemalettin Yılmaz Cd.-Sabri Mumcu Cd.-Inönü Blv.-Adnan Menderes Blv.-Şevki Hasırcı Meydanı-Candan Tarhan Blv.- Bahçearası Sk.- İnönü Blv. — 50. Yıl Cd.-Candan Tarhan Blv.- Gulhan Arın Blv- Saçıkara Sk- Enver Reis Sk-Hüseyin Reis Cd.-2. Sk.—4.Sk.

Dolmuş Routes 1-7

Dolmuş Number 3 Route

Kusadasi Hospital To Denizcilik Lisesi: Kusadası Devlet Hastanesi☐ Hülya Koçyiğit Cd.-Turgut Özal Blv.-422 Sk.-Dursun Akçam Cd.-422 Sk. —425 Sk.—438 Sk.-408 Sk.- Dursun Akçam Cd. -421 Sk.-408 Sk. —41 7 Sk.—4 1 8 Sk.-419 Sk.-424 Sk.-Turgut Özal Blv.-Adnan Menderes Blv.-Candan Tarhan Blv.—Gençlik Cd.-Aıatürk Blv.- İnönü Blv.-Adnan Menderes Blv.—Süleyman Demirel Blv.—Otogar Kavsağından dönüş☐ Süleyman Demirel Blv.-Turgut ÖzalBlv.—402 Sk.-Aydın Blv.—Güneş Sk.-Çamlıca Konakları-611 Sk.- Kırmızı Gül Yapı Koop.-611 Sk.- 613 Sk. —Kirazlı Yolu-Denizcilik Lisesi- Göcek Kavsağı-598 Sokak (Last Stop)

Dolmuş Routes 1-7

Dolmuş Number 4 Route

Denizcilik Lisesi To Kuşadası Devlet Hospital: Denizcilik LisesiGöcek Kavsağı -598 Sk.—Kirazlı Yolu-613 Sk.- Kırmızı Gül Yapı Koop.-611 Sk.-Çamlıbel Sitesi-Güneş Sk.-Aydın Blv.-Adnan Menderes Blv.—Candan Tarhan Blv.-Rıza Saraç Cd.- Atatürk Blv.-İnönü Blv.-Adnan Menderes Blv.-Süleyman Demirel Blv.—Otogar Kavsağından Dönüş-Süleyman Demirel Blv,- Turgut Özal Blv.—418 Sk.-417 Sk.-4088k.—421 Sk.-408 Sk.-438 Sk.-425 Sk- 442 Sk.-Dursun Akçam Cd.-Yalıkent Yapı Koop.- Turgut Özal Blv.-Hulya Kocyigit Cd.- Kusadası Devlet Hastanesi

Dolmuş Routes 1-7

Dolmuş Number 5 Route

Bahçelievleri Sitesi To Ladies Beach: Hüseyin Can Cd.—18 Sk.-Palmin Sunset-18 Sk.-14 Sk.-Yüksel Yalova Cd.— Kerner Cd.-Altın Kaynak Cd. 4. Sk.-Ölmez Evler l. Sk.-Enver Bıçakçı Cd. ı$ht. Üst Tğmn Cemalettin Yılmaz Cd.- Otogar Kavsağı-Süleyman Demirel Blv.-Adnan Menderes Blm—Candan Tarhan Bleahçearası Sk.-İnönü Blv.-50+ Yıl Cd.-Candan Tarhan Blv.—Rıza Saraç Cd.- Atatürk Blv.- M. Esat Bozkurt Cd.-Guvercinada Cd.- Kadınlar Denizi Cd.-Muharrem Candaş Sk.-9. Sk-15. Sk—16. Sk- Kadınlar Denizi (Last Stop)

Ladies Beach To Bahçelievleri Sitesi: Kadınlar Denizi I6. Sk.—15.Sk.-9, Sk.-ŞhtBaşkomiser Yaşar Aykaç Sk.-10. Sk.-Hamit Kaplan Sk.-Gazanfer Bilge Sk.-Yaşar Doğu Sk.-Kadınlar Denizi Cd.-Güvercinada Cdr—M.EsatBozkurt Cd.-Atatürk Blv.-İnönü Blv.-Adnan Menderes Blv.-Süleyman Demirel Blv.—Shl. Üst Tğmn+ Cemalettin Yılmaz Cd.-Kadınlar Denizi Yolu—Ölmez Evler l. Sk.-Altın Kaynak Cd. 4. Sk.- Kemer Cd.-Yüksel Yalova Cd.- 14. Sk.-18. Sk.—Palmin Sunset—18. Sk.—Hüseyin Can Cd.

Dolmuş Routes 1-7

Dolmuş Number 6 Route

Sahil Sitesi To Kusadasi Hospital: Nazilli Sitesi Kara SIL-Kadife Kalesi Sk.-Limon Sk.—Kara Sk.-Akdeniz Otel Yolu Sk.- -Ali Sah Sitesi-Öncü Sitesi-Deniz Yolu Cd.-Mustafa Birden Sk.Gözde Kent Sitesi-Karaova Sk.- Sağlık Cd.-Orhangazi Cd.— Çamlık Cd.—Süleyman Demirel Blv.-Kipa Kavşağından Dönüş—Süleyman Demirel Blv.+ Adnan Menderes Blv.- Candan Tarhan Blv.-.-Rıza Saraç Cd.-Aıalürk Blv-Okul Sokak-Gençlik Cd,-Candan Tarhan Blv.-Gülhan Arın Blv.-Turgut Özal Blv.-

Kusadası Devlet Hospital To Nazilli Sitesi: Hülya Koçyiğit Cd.-Atatürk Blv.-İnönü Blv.-Adnan Menderes Blv.-Süleyman Demirel Blv.-Kipa Avm'den Dönüş-Orhangazi Cd.-Çamlık Cd.- Sağlık Cd.-Karaova Sk.-Mustafa Birden Sk.—Deniz yolu Cd.- Akdeniz Ote-k yolu Sk.-Kara Sokak-Limon Sokak-Kadı Kalesi Sokak-Kara Sokak. Nazilli Sitesi. (Last Stop)

134

Dolmuş Routes 1-7

Dolmuş Number 7 Route

Sahil Sitesi To Kusadası Devlet Hospital: Nazilli Sitesi Kara Sk.-Nazilli Sitesi küme Evleri-Güneş Tur Siteei- Kuşadası/Davutlar Yolu-Süleyman Demirel Blv.-Uydukent Sitesi-Süleyman Demirel Blv.- Şht. Üst Tğmn Cemalettin Yılmaz Cd.-Sabri Mumcu Cd.-İnönü Blv.-Adnan Menderes Blv.-Candan Tarhan Blv.-Gençlik Caddesi-Okul Sk.— Atatürk Blv.- İnönü Blv.-50. Yıl Cd.—Candan Tarhan Blv.-Gülhan Arın Blv.-Turgul Özal Blv.- Kuşadası Devlet Hastanesi-

Kusadası Devlet Hospital To Nazilli Sitesi Kara Sokak: - Hülya Koç Yiğit Caddesi-Atatürk Blv: İnönü HIV,-Adnan Menderes Blv.-Süleyman Demirel Blv.-Uydukent Sitesi.- Süleyman Demirel Blv. Kusadası/Davutlar Yolu-Nazilli Sitesi Kara Sokak (Last Stop)

TAXIS

Taxis, while more expensive than the dolmuş, offer another convenient mode of transportation in Kusadası. They are especially handy during the peak tourist season when the minibuses might be crowded, or for late-night rides when the dolmuş service is less frequent. Kusadası's taxis are available around the clock and can provide a swift and comfortable journey to your destination.

In essence, Kusadası's local transportation system is well-designed to cater to the needs of its residents and visitors. Whether you prefer the economical and sociable experience of the dolmus or the private comfort ofa taxi, getting around Kusadası is easy, affordable, and convenient.

14.4 Moving to Kusadası

Making the move to live in Kusadası, Turkey, gives you permanent access to this wonderful city, that straddles history and modernity.

As a new resident, you have the choice of either renting or buying a home. Renting offers flexibility and less financial commitment, providing an excellent opportunity to familiarise yourself with the area, its culture, and neighbourhoods before settling down permanently.

On the other hand, buying a property is an appealing choice for those seeking long-term investment and stability. Kusadası's property market has a diverse range of homes, from apartments in the city centre to sea-view villas on the outskirts, providing options to suit every lifestyle and budget.

If you decide to rent keep in mind under the current law from most countries as a tourist you can stay in Turkey for 90 days in any 180 days period. However, if you buy a property worth more than $200,000 you can obtain a renewable residence permit for up to 2 years. Turkey also has a CIP (Citizenship Investment Programme) that allows you Turkish Citizenship by investing $400,000 into a property that can only be sold after a period of 3 years.

Renting a property in Turkey

Renting a property in Turkey can be an exciting new chapter in your life. By being thorough, informed, and proactive, you can make sure that you have a pleasant and hassle-free experience.

It's important to pay attention to four key areas before signing a rental agreement in Turkey.

Let's explore these areas in detail:

Rental contract: what to include

A well-drafted rental contract provides clarity and protects the interests of both the tenant and the landlord.

Here are some essential elements to include:

- **Identity information:** Ensure that the contract clearly states the details of both parties involved.
- **Property information**: Specify the location of the rented place, including the district, avenue, street, and door number.
- **Dates and duration:** Clearly define the start date and duration of the rental agreement to avoid any confusion.
- **Rental price and payment method**: Outline the agreed-upon rental price and specify the preferred payment method.

- **Conditions and usage:** Detail the conditions and rules for using the rented place, ensuring both parties are aware of their responsibilities.

- **Included assets:** If the lease includes any fixed assets, such as furniture or appliances, make sure they are listed in the contract..

Points to consider during the property search

Finding the right property requires careful consideration

Here are some factors to keep in mind:

- **Personal visit:** It is highly recommended to visit the property in person before making a decision. This allows you to assess its condition and suitability for your needs.

- **Surroundings:** Explore the neighbourhood to ensure it meets your preferences in terms of amenities, safety, and accessibility.
- **Repairs and maintenance:** Thoroughly inspect the property for any damages or areas in need of repair. Discuss these issues with the landlord before finalising the agreement.

- **Rental terms:** Pay attention to rental amount, rental increase rate, contract duration, and deposit amount. In Turkey, the deposit is typically equal to one month's rent and cannot exceed three times the monthly rental price.

- **Property handover:** Understand your obligations as a tenant to return the property in the same condition it was received. Any significant damages may result in deductions from the deposit.

Rental contract

Important questions to ask the owner

To avoid surprises later on, consider asking the following questions before committing to a rental property:

- **Utility expenses:** Clarify whether electricity, heating, and water expenses are included in the rental amount.

-

- **Owner's belongings:** If the property is furnished, inquire about any belongings of the owner that will remain in the house during your tenancy.

- **Personalisation:** Seek permission before making any changes like painting or adding decorations.

-

- **Pets policy:** If you have or plan to have a pet, inquire about the landlord's policy on pets.

- **Maintenance responsibilities:** Understand who is responsible for the maintenance and upkeep of the property.

- **Monthly fees:** Inquire about any additional monthly fees and whether they are already included in the rent.

- **Parking availability:** If you own a car, check if there is private or street parking available for your convenience.

Actions to take after moving in

Once you've secured your new home, there are important tasks to complete:

- **Official registrations**: Apply to authorised institutions, such as electricity, water, natural gas, and telephone providers, to transfer the subscriptions to your name at the start of the rental agreement.

- **Closing subscriptions:** Close any subscriptions at your previous residence and transfer your home insurance policies, if applicable, to your new home.

- **Address registration:** Notify the District Population Directorates within 30 days and the Provincial Immigration Administration within 20 days to register your new address.

- **Earthquake insurance:** Remember that it is mandatory for every home in Turkey to have compulsory Earthquake Insurance (DASK), and the responsibility lies with the landlord.

Remember, renting a property is not just about finding a place to live; it's about creating a comfortable and safe home for yourself. By paying attention to the details mentioned above, you can avoid potential misunderstandings, financial issues, and legal complications

Additionally, it's always a good idea to maintain open and friendly communication with the landlord or property owner. Building a positive relationship can help address any concerns or repairs promptly, ensuring a peaceful living arrangement.

When it comes to renting in Turkey, the property market offers a variety of options, depending on your preferences and budget. Take your time to explore different neighbourhoods and consider factors such as proximity to amenities, transportation links, and the overall atmosphere of the area.

Furthermore, familiarize yourself with local rental laws and regulations to understand your rights and responsibilities as a tenant. It's always wise to consult with a legal professional or a reputable estate agent who can guide you through the process and provide valuable insights.

Lastly, don't forget to trust your instincts and intuition when making decisions. If something feels off or raises concerns during your property search or interactions with the landlord, it's essential to address them and seek clarification before finalising any agreements

Purchasing a property in Kusadası: a straightforward and secure process

If you're considering buying a property in Kusadası, you'll find that the process is relatively straightforward. However, it's crucial to exercise caution and seek legal assistance, despite the claims of some estate agents who may advise against it.

Let's delve into the step-by-step process of purchasing a property in Kusadası or any other area of Turkey.

1.Obtain a tax number: To kickstart the process, you'll need to obtain a tax number from the local tax office. It's a simpleprocedure that involves visiting the tax office in Kusadası, locatednext to the cemetery, with your passport and a photocopy of it. Complete the required form, providing your personal details as well as the names of your parents. Once submitted, you'll receive your tax number immediately.

2.Open a bank account: With your tax number and passport, along with a utility bill (which can be from your home country), you can proceed to open a bank account. Having a Turkish bank account is essential for smooth financial transactions during the property purchase.

3.Partner with a reputable estate agent: The search for your ideal home is an exciting phase and a trustworthy estate agent is vital. Take some time to clearly define your preferences and requirements, such as the desired number of rooms, bathrooms, views, and amenities. It's helpful to create a wish list that outlines your expectations. Sharing these details with your agent will aid them in identifying suitable properties that align with your needs and budget. While it may not be possible to fulfil every item on your wish list, a reliable agent will do their best to find options that meet your criteria.

4.Engage a lawyer: When you've found your dream home, it's essential to engage a lawyer. The significance of legal representation cannot be overstated. Your lawyer will draft acontract that outlines the terms of the sale. At this stage, a deposit is typically paid to secure the property. The contract will specify the payment method, including the dates when payments are due.

Your lawyer will conduct thorough checks to ensure the property's title is clear and free from any encumbrances. At this stage for foreigners purchasing the property, an expert report will be organised. Once satisfied with the title's cleanliness and a satisfactory expert report, your lawyer will proceed to apply for the transfer of the title deed at the Tapu Office (Title Deed Office), transferring ownership to the new buyer.

5.Sign the Tapu: At the designated time, both the buyer and the seller, or their representatives, will meet at the Tapu Office to sign the transfer of the Tapu (title deed). This step formally recognises the buyer as the new owner of the property.

6.Register for property tax: Following the successful transfer of the Tapu, your lawyer will inform the property department at the municipality and register you as the official owner of the property for property tax purposes. This step ensures compliance with local regulations and obligations.

It's important to note that most property transactions in Turkey are conducted in cash, with the bulk of the funds typically being paid on the day of the title deed transfer. It is also possible to do a bank transfer on the day of the title deed transaction.

By following this structured approach and working closely with a reputable estate agent and a competent lawyer, you can navigate the property-buying process in Kusadası with confidence and peace of mind. Remember to prioritise legal assistance and thoroughly review all documentation before making any financial commitments.

14.5 Language and communication: Turkish and beyond

As the official language of Turkey, Turkish is spoken by everyone, from the local residents to the vendors in markets and everyone in between. However, the town's thriving tourism industry has led to the adoption of several other languages, notably English and other popular European languages, particularly among those who interact directly with tourists.

Due to Kusadası's status as a popular tourist destination, you'll find that many locals, particularly those working in the hospitality sector, have a strong command of English. They're accustomed to assisting tourists and are often capable of communicating effectively in English. Similarly, individuals working in restaurants, shops, and popular tourist attractions often have a good grasp of English and other European languages, which makes communication easier for international travellers.

However, learning a few fundamental phrases in Turkish is not only a mark of respect towards the local culture, but it can also enhance your overall travel experience. Even basic phrases can go a long way in breaking the ice and fostering a connection with the locals.

Engaging with locals using their native language, even if it's just simple greeting or a thank you, often elicits warm smiles and more personalised interactions. It's these small connections that truly enrich your journey, making your Kusadası experience far more than just another holiday.

Some commonly used Turkish phrases that might be helpful

Turkish	English
Merhaba	Hello
Teşekkür ederim	Thank you
Lütfen	Please
Evet	Yes
Hayır	No
Benim adım	My name is...
Ne yapıyorsunuz?	What are you doing?
Tuvalet nerede?	Where is thebathroom?
Yardım edin!	Help
Bir bira, lütfen	A beer, please
Nerede...?	Where is…?
Ne zaman...?	When is...?
Ne kadar?	How much?
Hesap, lütfen	The bill, please
Bu ne?	What is this?
Nasılsınız?	How are you?
İyi	Good
Kötü	Bad
Büyük	Big
Küçük	Small
Aç	Hungry
Susuz	Thirsty
Biraz Türkçe konuşuyorum	I speak a little Turkish
Tekrar eder misiniz?	Can you repeat that?
İngilizce konuşuyor musunuz?	Do you speak English?
Acil durum	Emergency
Hastane	Hospital
Anlaşıldı	Understood
Afiyet olsun Bon appétit	Enjoy your meal

English & Turkish Numbers

1 = Bir	30 = Otuz
2 = İki	40 = Kırk
3 = Üç	50 = Elli
4 = Dört	60 = Altmış
5 = Beş	70 = Yetmiş
6 = Altı	80 = Seksen
7 = Yedi	90 = Doksan
8 = Sekiz	100 = Yüz
9 = Dokuz	200 = İki yüz
10 = On	300 = Üç yüz
11 = On bir	400 = Dört yüz
12 = On iki	500 = Beş yüz
13 = On üç	600 = Altı yüz
14 = On dört	700 = Yedi yüz
15 = On beş	800 = Sekiz yüz
16 = On altı	900 = Dokuz yüz
17 = On yedi	1000 = Bin
18 = On sekiz	2000 = İki Bin
19 = On dokuz	3000 = Üç Bin
20 = Yirmi	4000 = Dört Bin

14.6 Currency and money matters: the Turkish lira

The Turkish lira (TRY), the official currency of Kusadası and indeed the rest of Turkey, is what you'll be using throughout your stay in the city. Kusadası is well-equipped with financial amenities such as ATMs, making it easy for you to withdraw cash at any time. These machines are typically compatible with international banking systems, ensuring smooth transactions for foreign travellers.

Credit and debit cards are also widely accepted across Kusadası, especially in larger establishments such as hotels, upscale restaurants, and prominent retail outlets. This cashless convenience adds a layer of ease to your holiday, allowing you to enjoy your meals or shopping trips without the worry of carrying a large amount of cash.

However, despite the widespread card acceptance, it's wise to keep a fair amount of cash on hand. This is particularly true if you plan on venturing to the local markets and bazaars, or if you're dining at smaller, local eateries. Some of these places, especially in more traditional or rural areas, might not have card payment facilities or might prefer cash transactions. Also, for smaller purchases like a quick snack, a souvenir from a street vendor, or a ride in a dolmuş (shared minibus), cash is often the preferred or even the only acceptable form of payment.

Additionally, while exploring the rich culture of Kusadası, you may come across talent ted street performers or wish to give a gratuity forgood service, both of which are situations where having some coins or small notes handy would be beneficial.

14.7 Banking in Turkey

The banking system in Turkey is characterised by a mix of private and state-owned banks, and it plays a central role in the Turkish economy. The system is well-regulated and supervised by the Banking Regulation and Supervision Agency (BRSA), ensuring a high standard of stability and security for customers. Banks in Turkey provide many services, ranging from retail and commercial banking to investment services and insurance products. They are also leading in the region in terms of digital banking services, as most Turkish banks offer online and mobile banking facilities.

The Turkish banking sector is known for its resilience. Despite occasional periods of economic instability, it has demonstrated impressive robustness, thanks in part to a stringent regulatory environment and substantial capital buffers.

A closer look at the Top 10 Banks in Turkey

1.Ziraat Bank: Established in 1863, Ziraat Bank is the largest and oldest state-owned bank in Turkey. Its vast branch network and strong capital base make it a major player in the banking sector. The bank's services range from retail banking and SME financing to investment banking and treasury operations. With a customer-centric approach, Ziraat Bank continues to innovate, promoting financial inclusion and sustainable growth.

2.Garanti BBVA: Garanti BBVA, a member of the Spanish banking group BBVA, is a leading private bank in Turkey, known for its digital banking advancements. Garanti offers a wide array of services, including retail banking, corporate banking, and SME banking. With a focus on innovation and sustainability, it continues to serve millions of customers with unique products and services.

3.Akbank: Akbank, founded in 1948, is another leading privatebank with strong ties to the Turkish industrial sector. Known for its superior customer service and robust corporate banking operations, Akbank has an extensive domestic and international network. Its innovative approach has allowed it to pioneer in areas such as digital banking and mobile banking services.

4.İş Bank: This bank, established in 1924, has historically played a crucial role in Turkey's development. İş Bank provides a comprehensive range of banking services, including investment banking, SME banking, and retail banking. The bank has a broad network of branches both in Turkey and abroad, supporting its diverse customer base.

5.Yapı Kredi Bank: A joint venture between Koc Holding and UniCredit, Yapı Kredi Bank has a strong reputation for high- quality service. The bank offers a full range of financial services, such as retail banking, private banking, and asset management. Its significant presence in credit card and non- cash transactions market reflects its innovation in consumer banking.

6.Halkbank: Established in 1938, Halkbank is a state-owned bank primarily serving the needs of small and medium-sized enterprises (SMEs). It offers deposit and investment services, loans, insurance products, and pension fund management. The bank also provides international banking services, contributing to Turkey's foreign trade and economic development.

7.VakıfBank: Another state-owned bank, VakıfBank has played a significant role in supporting Turkey's public and private sector investments. VakıfBank's offerings include retail, corporate, and SME banking services. It has recently increased its focus on digital transformation and is known for its strong customer satisfaction scores.

8.QNB Finansbank: Owned by Qatar National Bank, QNB Finansbank is a major private bank that provides a comprehensive range of banking services. It has a strong presence in retail banking and is known for its excellent customer service, competitive loan rates, and technologically advanced banking solutions.

9.DenizBank: Founded in 1997 and owned by Emirates NBD, DenizBank offers retail banking, private banking, and business banking services. Known for its digital banking solutions, the bank has earned a reputation as a leader in technological innovation within Turkey's banking sector. It has a diverse range of offerings, from traditional banking products to alternative channels like mobile banking and ATMs.

10.TEB (Türk Ekonomi Bankası): Part of the BNP Paribas Group, TEB offers a range of innovative financial services. It has a strong presence in business banking and stands out for its commitment to supporting SMEs. TEB's innovative products and digital banking services make it a competitive player in the Turkish banking industry.

Each of these banks provides a unique combination of services, making Turkey's banking sector one of the most dynamic in the world. These institutions contribute significantly to the country's financial system, catering to the needs of a broad range of customers and businesses, and playing a crucial role in Turkey's economic growth and stability.

14.8 The rise of medical tourism in Kusadasi Turkey

In the landscape of international healthcare, Turkey has been steadily making a name for itself, especially in the niche of medical tourism. Today, it stands as a sought-after destination for dental treatments, hair transplants, and aesthetic procedures, offering world-class medical services at a fraction of the cost compared to Europe and the United States.

Turkey's medical tourism market is shaped by several factors. State-of-the-art medical facilities, highly-trained and English-speaking medical professionals, and an impressive regulatory environment have made the country a safe and attractive option. But what truly sets Kusadası apart is its innovative approach to blending tourism and healthcare, presenting an affordable yet fulfilling experience.

Dental Treatments

Dental treatments in Kusadası are particularly popular among medical tourists. The city boasts an array of excellent dental clinics, equipped with cutting-edge technology and expert dental professionals. What's more, the cost of dental care here is impressively competitive— prices can be up to 70% cheaper than in Western countries. This significant difference does not compromise the quality of the service provided. From basic dental check-ups and fillings to more complex procedures like implants and veneers, patients have expressed a high level of satisfaction with the care received.

Dental Treatments

Hair Transplantation

Kusadası is also making waves in the field of hair transplantation. A procedure that could cost thousands of dollars in the US or Europe can be performed in Kusadası at a much lower rate. These procedures are carried out by skilled surgeons who employ the latest techniques, ensuring both safety and efficacy.

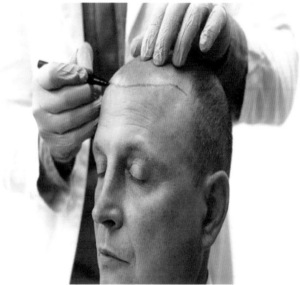

Hair Transplantation

Aesthetic Treatments

Aesthetic treatments, too, have found a home in Kusadası. The city offers a variety of services such as laser treatments, dermal fillers, chemical peels, and much more. Again, cost-effectiveness is the highlight, attracting many who seek to combine a vacation with self-enhancement.

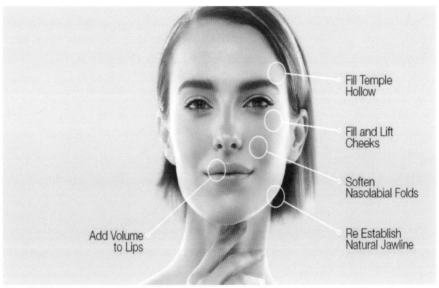

Fill Temple Hollow

Fill and Lift Cheeks

Soften Nasolabial Folds

Add Volume to Lips

Re Establish Natural Jawline

Aesthetic treatments

Kusadası's popularity in the medical tourism field is a testament to its unique blend of top-notch medical care, affordable prices, and the opportunity to recover in a stunning tourist destination. It is a confluence of wellness and leisure that few places can offer.

It is clear that Kusadası is reshaping the narrative of medical tourism. Offering a diverse range of treatments at prices that make quality healthcare accessible to many more people, it truly exemplifies the beneficial synergy of healthcare and tourism. It is not just a city where one can receive excellent medical care, but also a place where patients can heal amidst natural beauty and cultural richness.

14.9 Health and safety: staying safe in Kusadası

Kusadası, like many places in Turkey, is generally considered a safe and welcoming destination for tourists from around the globe. The locals are known for their hospitality and warmth, often going out of their way to make visitors feel at home. That said, safety should always be a priority when travelling, and Kusadası is no exception to this rule.

As you immerse yourself in the town's culture, it's essential to remain vigilant and take some common-sense precautions. Safeguarding your belongings is one such precaution. Always keep your personal items close, and consider using a hotel safe for valuables like passports, tickets, and expensive electronics when you're out and about exploring the town.

While the town is quite safe to navigate, it is advisable to avoid poorly lit or deserted areas late at night, especially if you are alone. Stick to well populated areas and follow the same safety principles you would use in any other city around the world.

In the unlikely event that you are approached by someone who makes you feel uncomfortable, it's best to trust your instincts and remove yourself from the situation. If necessary, seek assistance from local authorities or your hotel staff.

Kusadası is also prepared for health-related concerns. The town is home to several hospitals and medical centres equipped with modern facilities, providing high-quality healthcare services. Many doctors and healthcare professionals in Kusadası have received international training, and it is not uncommon to find English-speaking staff in many healthcare facilities.

Pharmacies, known locally as 'Eczane', are also conveniently located throughout the town, and they stock a good range of over-the- counter and prescription medications. In many cases, pharmacists can provide helpful advice and minor ailment services.

Travel insurance is highly recommended for all tourists. Ensure that your policy covers any activities you plan to engage in, whether that's sailing, hiking, or simply exploring the town's historical sites.

Essentially, while Kusadası is a friendly and generally safe town, maintaining awareness and taking preventative measures will ensure yourtrip is a pleasant and memorable one.

Conclusion

Reflecting on Kusadası's timeless charm

As we draw our exploration of Kusadası to a close, a sense of enchantment permeates our reflections, sparked by the timeless charm that this corner of Turkey so effortlessly exudes. Kusadası, with its perfect blend of ancient heritage and modern pleasures, sun-kissed beaches and busy markets, offers a plethora of unforgettable experiences for every traveller who steps foot on its welcoming shores.

Our journey has allowed us to delve deep into the heart of the town's rich tapestry of history and culture, revealing an intriguing blend of East and West, old and new. We've roamed through ancient ruins that echo with the whispers of centuries past, each stone and artefact narrating a tale more captivating than the last. We've witnessed the architectural grandeur of the Byzantine and Ottoman eras, their influence still so palpable in the town's atmospheric streets and buildings.

The sun-soaked beaches of Kusadası, with their golden sands and turquoise waters, have beckoned us time and again, offering the promise of relaxation and rejuvenation. The gentle murmur of the Aegean Sea has provided the perfect soundtrack to our idyllic beachside sojourns, as we've basked in the warmth of the Mediterranean sun, savoured the cool sea breeze, and enjoyed the mesmerising views of the endless blue horizon.

Our ventures beyond the town's limits have taken us through verdant national parks, where nature's bounty has left us in awe. We've discovered the captivating beauty of the surrounding islands, each one a little piece of paradise waiting to be explored. These excursions have further enriched our Kusadası experience, reminding us of the diverse and stunning landscapes that Turkey has to offer.

And of course, who could forget our gastronomic adventures in Kusadası? We've immersed ourselves in the local culinary scene, sampling mouthwatering dishes that celebrate the flavours of the Aegean. From food markets to fine-dining establishments, we've tasted our way through the region's cuisine, each bite a testament to the culinary prowess and passion of the local chefs.

In essence, Kusadası is more than just a tourist destination—it is a meeting point of history and culture, natural beauty and gastronomic delights. As we reflect on our journey, we are left with not just memories, but also a deeper appreciation for this fascinating Aegean town and its timeless charm.

Visit and experience Kusadası firsthand

While this comprehensive guide to Kusadası has endeavoured to capture the essence of this enchanting town and provide useful insights into its many attractions, it is but a primer to the magic that awaits when you come to visit. The true allure of Kusadası is best experienced firsthand, as you navigate through its lively streets, immerse yourself in its rich history, and soak up its colourful culture. Whether you're planning your maiden voyage to this coastal town, or preparing for yet another rendezvous with its many charms, we encourage you to embark on your personal adventure with an open heart and an explorer's spirit.

Our hope is that this guidebook serves as more than a mere source of practical information for your travels. We aspire for it to kindle a passion within you for Kusadası—a flame that will burn brightly, long after your visit. As you embark on your own Kusadası journey, may you create treasured memories that will keep you warm in years to come. May every step taken, every vista beheld, and every interaction fostered in this charming town, find a special place in your heart, as they have for countless travellers who have come before.

**If you have any questions please feel free to contact me:
moni@KusadasiLife.net**

162

Useful Telephone Numbers

Emergency Services:

Police emergency: 155
New single number for all emergencies: 112
Coast Guard: 158

Medical Services:

Kusadası State Hospital: +90 256 618 24 14

Tourist Information:

Kusadası Tourism Information Office: +90 256 614 11 03
Kusadası Municipality Guvercin Masa: +90 256 460 40 40

Transportation:

Kusadası Bus Terminal: +90 256 614 39 81
Kusadası dolmuş (Minibus) Station: +90 256 614 13 73

Embassy/Consulate:

British Embassy in Ankara: (Consular Services): +90 312 455 33 44
U.S. Embassy in Ankara: (US Citizen Services): +90 312 455 55 55
Canadian Embassy in Ankara: (Consular Services): +90 312 409 27 00
Australian Embassy in Ankara: (Consular Services): +90 312 459 95 00
Kuwait Embassy in Ankara: (Consular Services) +90 312 445 05 76
Belgian Embassy in Ankara: (Consular Services) +90 312 405 61 66

Please note that telephone numbers can change over time, so it's always a good idea to double-check the numbers before your visit or save the local emergency numbers on your mobile phone for quick access.

About Author

Moni Arora, the trailblazing force behind the popular YouTube Channel @KusadasıLife, has been a digital storyteller and ambassador of the Aegean lifestyle since the channel's inception. Hailing from an eclectic background with expertise in various fields, Moni is well-known for his enthralling narratives and vivid portrayals of life in the Turkish town of Kusadası. His passion for the region, its culture, and its people is evident in his compelling content which explores Kusadası's multi-faceted charm.

A keen observer of life, Moni's roots in storytelling extend beyond the digital landscape, with his latest work, "Aegean Whispers: Kusadası's Charm," taking readers on a breathtaking journey through the enchanting town. The book encapsulates Kusadası's spirit and the Aegean lifestyle mystique

Moni's unique perspective as an outsider-turned-local has won the hearts and admiration of the community. He provides an engaging and personal lens into the Aegean lifestyle, making distant cultures feel incredibly close. Moni Arora is an inspirational figure who embodies a ceaseless spirit of exploration, a deep reverence for culture and history, and an exceptional talent for storytelling.

Check out Kusadasi Life YouTube Channel @KusadasiLife

164

Printed in Poland
by Amazon Fulfillment
Poland Sp. z o.o., Wrocław

33136926R00098